Table of Contents

Practice Test #1

Practice Questions

Reading Skills and Knowledge

Questions 1-9 pertain to the following passage:

OPPOSITIONAL DEFIANT DISORDER

On a bad day, have you ever been irritable? Have you ever used a harsh tone or even been verbally disrespectful to your parents or teachers? Everyone has a short temper from time to time, but current statistics indicate that between 16% and 20% of a school's population suffer from a psychological condition known as <u>Oppositional</u> Defiance Disorder, or ODD.

ODD symptoms include difficulty complying with adult requests, excessive arguments with adults, temper tantrums, difficulty accepting responsibility for actions, <u>low frustration tolerance</u>, and behaviors intended to annoy or upset adults. Parents of children with ODD can often feel as though their whole relationship is based on conflict after conflict.

Unfortunately, ODD can be caused by a number of factors. Some students affected by ODD suffer abuse, neglect, and severe or unpredictable discipline at home. Others have parents with mood disorders or have experienced family violence. Various types of therapy are helpful in treating ODD, and some drugs can treat particular symptoms. However, no single cure exists.

The best advice from professionals is directed toward parents. Therapists encourage parents to avoid situations that usually end in power struggles, to try not to <u>feed into</u> oppositional behavior by reacting emotionally, to praise positive behaviors, and to discourage negative behaviors with timeouts instead of harsh discipline.

1. Which of the following statements can be inferred from paragraph 4?
   a. Parents of children with ODD are bad parents.
   b. ODD is not a real psychological disorder.
   c. Medication can worsen ODD.
   d. Reacting emotionally to defiant behavior might worsen the behavior.

2. Which of the following best describes the main idea of this passage?
   a. ODD has no cause.
   b. ODD is a complex condition.
   c. Parents with ODD should seek support.
   d. Parents are the cause of ODD.

- 4 -

3. As used in this passage, the word <u>oppositional</u> most nearly means:
    a. Uncooperative
    b. Violent
    c. Passive aggressive
    d. Altruistic

4. Which of the following can be inferred from paragraph one?
    a. Most children who speak harshly to their parents have ODD.
    b. Most people exhibit symptoms of ODD occasionally.
    c. Between 16% and 20% of the school population has been abused.
    d. A short temper is a symptom of obsessive compulsive disorder.

5. As used in this passage, the phrase <u>feed into</u> most nearly means:
    a. Discourage
    b. Ignore
    c. Encourage
    d. Abuse

6. As used in this passage, the phrase <u>low frustration tolerance</u> most nearly means:
    a. Patience
    b. Low IQ
    c. Difficulty dealing with frustration
    d. The ability to cope with frustration

7. The author's purpose in writing this passage is to:
    a. Express frustration about ODD.
    b. Prove that parents are the cause of ODD.
    c. Inform the reader about this complex condition.
    d. Persuade the reader to keep students with ODD out of public school.

8. According to the passage, which of the following is a cause of ODD?
    a. Excessive television viewing.
    b. Poor diet.
    c. Severe or unpredictable punishment.
    d. Low IQ.

9. Based on the passage, which of the following statements seems most true?
    a. A variety of parenting techniques can be used to help children with ODD.
    b. Children with ODD must be physically aggressive to be diagnosed.
    c. Parents of children with ODD often engage in risk-taking activities.
    d. Harsh disciplinary measures must be used to control children with ODD.

Questions 10-18 pertain to the following passage:

EARLY POLITICAL PARTIES

The United States has always been a <u>pluralistic</u> society, meaning it has always embraced many points of view and many groups with different identities. That is not to say that these groups have always seen eye to eye. The first political parties developed in the United States as a result of conflicting visions of the American identity. Many politicians believed that wealthy merchants and lawyers represented the country's true identity, but many others saw <u>it</u> in the farmers and workers who formed the country's economic base.

The event that brought this disagreement to the surface was the creation of the Bank of the United States in 1791. The bank set out to rid the country of the debts it had accumulated during the American Revolution. Until then, each state was responsible for its own debts. The Bank of the United States, however, wanted to assume these debts and pay them off itself. While many people considered this offer to be a good financial deal for the states, many states were uncomfortable with the arrangement because they saw it as a power play by the federal government. If a central bank had control over the finances of individual states, the people who owned the bank would profit from the states in the future. This concern was the basis of the disagreement: Who should have more power, the individual states or the central government?

The Democratic-Republican Party developed to protest the bank, but it came to represent a vision of America with power spread among states. The Federalist Party was established in defense of the bank, but its ultimate vision was of a strong central government that could help steer the United States toward a more <u>competitive</u> position in the world economy.

These different points of view—central government versus separate states—would not be resolved easily. These same disagreements fueled the tension that erupted into the Civil War over half a century later.

10. According to the passage, the word "pluralistic" most nearly means:
    a. Divisive
    b. Conservative
    c. Tolerant
    d. Liberty

11. What is the author's purpose in writing this passage?
    a. To persuade the reader to accept the Federalist Party's point of view.
    b. To explain the disagreements between early American political parties.
    c. To explain the importance of a strong central government.
    d. To criticize the founders of the Bank of the United States.

12. The word "competitive" is used in the passage to mean:
    a. Inferior
    b. Stronger
    c. Partisan
    d. Identity

13. Which of the following best describes the main idea of the passage?
    a. Political parties should emphasize areas of agreement instead of disagreement.
    b. The earliest political parties in the U.S. reflected conflicting interests.
    c. The Federalist Party had a better plan for the America's interests abroad.
    d. The Bank of the United States was not a secure financial institution.

14. In the last sentence of the first paragraph, the pronoun "it" refers to which of the following?
    a. The country's identity.
    b. The future of the country.
    c. State's rights.
    d. A political party.

15. Which of the following statements can be inferred from the second paragraph?
    a. The formation of the Bank of the United States should not have created so much conflict.
    b. Individual states believed that they should not have to share their profits with the central government.
    c. The bank was attempting to swindle the states.
    d. The states were not willing to listen to reason.

16. Which of the following statements best fits with the viewpoint of the Federalist Party?
    a. The U.S. should be a confederacy of individual states with equal power.
    b. The government should not meddle in the affairs of states.
    c. States should not have any rights.
    d. The stronger the central government, the stronger the country.

17. Which of the following statements best fits with the viewpoint of the Democratic-Republican Party?
    a. The federal government should not have too much power.
    b. The Bank of the United States would never be able to repay the states' debts.
    c. The states should not have too much power.
    d. The constitution must be revised to give the government more power.

18. Which of the following statements can be inferred from the final paragraph?
    a. The Civil War was fought between the Federalist and the Democratic-Republican Parties.
    b. The different interests reflected by the first two political parties were not easily reconciled.
    c. The Civil War could have been avoided if the Bank of the United States had not been created.
    d. The Bank of the United States is a direct cause of the Civil War.

Application of Reading Skills and Knowledge to Classroom Instruction

19. A high school English teacher asked the students to read a magazine article about the Uffizi Gallery in Florence, Italy, and its collection of Italian Renaissance paintings. The teacher advised the students to annotate the text with comments and questions. Later the students would discuss their respective annotations. What does Jason's comment indicate about what he learned?

> Jason's annotation: The Italian Renaissance produced some of the world's greatest masterpieces from the thirteenth to the sixteenth centuries.

    a. He understands the timeline of the historical period of the collection.
    b. He knows about the content of the paintings in the collection.
    c. He recognizes the names of the artists who did these paintings.
    d. He knows about the architecture of this museum.

20. Which of the following instructional strategies would help students recognize the text structures of comparison and contrast or cause and effect in a history textbook?
    a. defining the historical events occurring in a certain time period
    b. showing students how to recognize signal words such as similar to or instead of, which show these text structures
    c. providing a timeline of the period of history being discussed
    d. discussing the maps provided throughout the textbook

21. A history teacher discusses the structure of nonfiction texts by explaining the text structures of comparison and contrast, cause and effect, problem and solution, and chronological order. Which text structure do the following chapter titles from *A Textbook of the History of Architecture* represent?

> CHAPTER I: PRIMITIVE AND PREHISTORIC ARCHITECTURE
> CHAPTER X: .EARLY CHRISTIAN ARCHITECTURE
> CHAPTER XIII: EARLY MEDIAEVAL ARCHITECTURE IN ITALY AND FRANCE
> CHAPTER XX: EARLY RENAISSANCE ARCHITECTURE IN ITALY
> CHAPTER XXVII: ARCHITECTURE IN THE UNITED STATES

    a. comparison and contrast
    b. cause and effect
    c. chronological order
    d. problem and solution

22. Students read an article in a magazine about codebreaking. This article showed how sending secret messages has evolved from wrapping parchment with secret messages around sticks to secret messages embedded in pictures and music on the Internet. This article showed the students that the technology of hidden messages has
    a. remained the same through the years.
    b. decreased through the years.
    c. decreased in importance.
    d. increased through the years.

23. After the eleventh-grade students read the World War II story of the brave German theologian Dietrich Bonhoeffer, a Lutheran minister who defied Hitler, the teacher had students explain their personal definitions of faith. This activity is likely to benefit students PRIMARILY by

    a. introducing them to World War II.
    b. teaching them about Germany.
    c. involving them in the concept of faith.
    d. providing a multicultural true story.

24. An English teacher asked her students to choose a novel and prepare an oral presentation on the language and style of their selection. Josh read from the first chapter of *The Adventures of Tom Sawyer* by Mark Twain, and gave his report.

"TOM!"
    No answer.
"TOM!"
    No answer.
"What's gone with that boy, I wonder? You TOM!"
    No answer.
    The old lady pulled her spectacles down and looked over them about the room; then she put them up and looked out under them. She seldom or never looked *through* them for so small a thing as a boy; they were her state pair, the pride of her heart, and were built for "style," not service—she could have seen through a pair of stove-lids just as well. She looked perplexed for a moment, and then said, not fiercely, but still loud enough for the furniture to hear:
    "Well, I lay if I get hold of you I'll—"
    She did not finish, for by this time she was bending down and punching under the bed with the broom, and so she needed breath to punctuate the punches with. She resurrected nothing but the cat.

                           The Adventures of Tom Sawyer by Mark Twain

---

Josh reported the word choices in the passage he read to be

    a. colloquial.
    b. abstract.
    c. formal.
    d. allusive.

25. An English teacher asked the students to research the literary and rhetorical terms listed on the table, show examples from literature, and have a class discussion about the meanings of the terms.

Literary and Rhetorical Terms	
Allegory	Onomatopoeia
Alliteration	Oxymoron
Analogy	Paradox
Epigraph	Symbol
Hyperbole	Theme

The teacher's intent in having students research these terms would be to
    a. familiarize them with these literary and rhetorical terms.
    b. show the variety of language and style used in writing.
    c. generate interest in reading diverse materials.
    d. all of the above.

26. John, who always felt like a failure when his teacher asked him to revise his work, was surprised when a visiting author talked about the extensive revisions in her books. What did he learn from the visiting author's presentation that helped him to better accept his teacher's request for revisions?
    a. Revisions are rarely necessary.
    b. Revisions are a normal process in writing.
    c. Revisions show an inability to write a piece initially.
    d. Revisions do not improve writing.

27. The English teacher read a passage from contemporary YA novel that shows a student's conflict with her mother. The main character, Beth, takes a stand against her mother's demand that she participate in art rather than in science, her main interest. The teacher asked the students to remember a similar conflict they had with a parent or a sibling and write a brief paragraph about how they felt.
This exercise would address which of the following instructional goals?
    a. Encourage students to use writing as a means for personal exploration and self-expression.
    b. Encourage students to disagree with their parents or siblings on issues that might be important to them.
    c. Encourage students to understand the structure of a contemporary novel.
    d. Encourage students to understand how a plot is developed through conflict.

28. The English teacher read a statement by Benjamin Franklin and asked her students what made this writing so memorable.

> Early to bed and early to rise, makes a man healthy, wealthy, and wise.
> *Poor Richard's Almanack.* October 1735.

    a. use of alliteration
    b. use of parallel construction
    c. use of metaphors
    d. use of similes

29. The teacher asked the students to keep a log of their summer reading. Lee kept the following log of his first book.

Title/Author	Genre	Goal	Personal Challenge Level 1–10 Explain	Did I accomplish my goal?
The Legacy of Bletchley Park by Annie Laura Smith	Historical Fiction	I wanted to read a book that explained code breaking during World War II.	Level 5: I had trouble understanding why code breaking was so complex.	Yes, Gretchen's fluent German helped her to translate the decoded messages. Her participation at Bletchley Park showed me the code breaking process.

Which of the following literary strengths does Lee demonstrate in this entry?
    a. an understanding of plotting techniques used in this story
    b. an awareness of the value of conflict in this story
    c. an interest in what is involved in code breaking in this story
    d. an awareness of character development in this story

30. The teacher explained to the English class how to avoid plagiarism when writing an assignment. What did the teacher suggest that would BEST avoid plagiarism?
    a. Rewrite information from research materials significantly.
    b. Copy word-for-word and give attribution to research sources.
    c. Copy word-for-word to be accurate.
    d. Rewrite and give attribution to research sources.

Mathematics Skills and Knowledge

31. If an odd number is added to an even number, the result must be
    a. odd
    b. even
    c. positive
    d. zero

32. Which of the following is equal to 6.19×10^3?
    a. .00619
    b. .0619
    c. 619
    d. 6,190

33. What is the area of a square with perimeter 16 ft?
    a. 4 ft2
    b. 16 ft2
    c. 32 ft2
    d. 256 ft^2

34. Which of the following is equal to $4\sqrt{2^4}$?
   a. 4
   b. 8
   c. 16
   d. 32

35. A class contains an equal number of boys and girls. The average height of the boys is 62 inches. The average height of the all the students is 60 inches. What is the average height of the girls in the class?
   a. 57 inches
   b. 58 inches
   c. 59 inches
   d. 60 inches

36. A circle has an area equal to 36π. What is its diameter?
   a. 4
   b. 6
   c. 12
   d. 4π

37. A dartboard is divided into 8 black and 8 white wedge-shaped sectors, so that when a dart is thrown it has a 50% chance of landing on white, and a 50% chance of landing on black. If a dart is thrown 3 times in a row and lands on black each time, what is the chance that it will land again on black if it is thrown a fourth time?
   a. 12.5%
   b. 25%
   c. 50%
   d. 100%

38. How many integers exist between the numbers -4.2 and +6.1?
   a. 2
   b. 6
   c. 10
   d. 11

39. Which of the following expressions represents "five times a number m squared"?
   a. $\dfrac{5}{m^2}$
   b. $5m^2$
   c. $(5m)^2$
   d. $5 + m^2$

40. The radius of a circle with an area of 31 square units is doubled. What is the area of the new circle?
   a. 62 square units
   b. 93 square units
   c. 124 square units
   d. 132 square units

41. If $3x + 5 = 11$, then $x = ?$
   a. 6
   b. 3
   c. 2
   d. 1

42. Rachel spent $24.15 on vegetables. She bought 2 pounds of onions, 3 pounds of carrots, and 1 ½ pounds of mushrooms. If the onions cost $3.69 per pound, and the carrots cost $4.29 per pound, what is the price per pound of mushrooms?
   a. $2.60
   b. $2.25
   c. $2.80
   d. $3.10

43. Which of these is a solution to the inequality $4x - 12 < 4$?
   a. $x < 2$
   b. $x > 2$
   c. $x > 4$
   d. $x < 4$

44. If $a = -6$ and $b = 7$, then $4a(3b + 5) + 2b = ?$
   a. 638
   b. -485
   c. 850
   d. -610

45. Mark is driving to Phoenix, a distance of 210 miles. He drives the first ten miles in 12 minutes. If he continues at the same rate, how long will it take him to reach his destination?
   a. 3 hours 15 minutes
   b. 4 hours 12 minutes
   c. 3 hours 45 minutes
   d. 4 hours 20 minutes

46. An airplane leaves Atlanta at 2 PM and flies north at 250 miles per hour. A second airplane leaves Atlanta 30 minutes later and flies north at 280 miles per hour. At what time will the second airplane overtake the first?
   a. 6:00 PM
   b. 6:20 PM
   c. 6:40 PM
   d. 6:50 PM

47. The table shows the cost of renting a bicycle for 1, 2, or 3 hours. Which of the following equations best represents the data, if C represents the cost and h represents the time of the rental?

Hours	1	2	3
Cost	$3.60	$7.20	$10.80

   a. $C = 3.60h$
   b. $C = h + 3.60$
   c. $C = 3.60h + 10.80$
   d. $C = 10.80/h$

48. Chan receives a bonus from his job. He pays 30% in taxes, gives 30% to charity, and uses another 25% to pay off an old debt. He has $600 left. What was the total amount of Chan's bonus?

    a. $4000

    b. $3600

    c. $3200

    d. $3000

Application of Mathematics Skills and Knowledge of Classroom Instruction

49. A student is presented with the following problem: $4^2 + 5(4 \times 3) - 10$. Which operation should the student perform first?

    a. Multiplying five by four and three

    b. Squaring four

    c. Subtracting ten from three

    d. Adding four and five

50. A student is asked to find the perimeter of a shape with four sides of different length. Which general equation suggests the calculation the student will need to perform?

    a. $P = 42$

    b. $P = x4$

    c. $P = a + b + c + d$

    d. $P = 2x + 2y$

51. Students are working on telling time. The teacher adjusts the hands of a clock and asks the students to say what time it is. One student says "ten two." To what time is the student probably referring?

    a. 2:02

    b. 2:10

    c. 10:10

    d. 10:02

52. Students are given the following word problem: "A man needs to make fifty cupcakes. Each of his baking trays will hold eight cupcakes. How many baking trays will the man need?" One student determines the answer to be 6.25. Why is this answer incorrect?

    a. The answer should be expressed as a mixed number.

    b. Baking trays cannot be subdivided.

    c. The student's arithmetic is incorrect.

    d. The student should round down to six.

53. A student is asked to find 3/5 of 75. Which of the following expressions could the student use?

    a. $(3 \times 75) \div 5$

    b. $75 \div 0.6$

    c. Either A or B

    d. Neither A nor B

54. Students are given the following algebra problem: $2x + 5 = 20$. One student comes up an answer of $x = 12.5$. Is the student correct and, if not, what has the student most likely done wrong?

    a. Yes, the student's answer is incorrect.

    b. No, the student has not rounded up to 13.

    c. No, the student has probably not divided both sides by two.

    d. No, the student has most likely added five to both sides rather than subtracting.

55. $4(3 \times 7) \div 8 = ?$

A student created the above number sentence to solve the following problem:

"Divide the sum of the products of four and three and four and seven by eight."

What is the correct number sentence for this problem?

    a. $(4 + 3)(4 + 7) \div 8 = ?$

    b. $(4 \times 3)(4 \times 7) \div 8 = ?$

    c. $4(3 + 7) \div 8 = ?$

    d. The student's number sentence is correct.

56. Students are asked to add 3/8 and 5/6. What must be their first step?

    a. Finding the lowest common denominator

    b. Multiplying three by five

    c. Finding the greatest common factor

    d. Adding three and five

57. A student is asked to find the factors of 32. She comes up with the following list: 1, 2, 4, 8, 16, 32. Is this list correct?

    a. Yes, it includes all the factors of 32.

    b. Yes, but it omits several additional possible factors.

    c. No, it contains several terms that are not factors of 32.

    d. No, it is a list of the multiples rather than the factors of 32.

58. Students are presented with the following word problem:

"Five basketball teams participate in a round-robin tournament, where each team plays all of the other teams one time. How many games will be played in the tournament?"

Which equation could students use to solve this problem?

    a. $(5 \times 4) \div 2 = ?$

    b. $5 + 4 + 3 + 2 + 1 = ?$

    c. $4 \times 3 \times 2 \times 1 = ?$

    d. $5 \times 5 = ?$

59. Students are asked to list pairs of terms that have a ratio of 5:4. Which of these pairs should not be on the list?

    a. 25 and 20

    b. 15 and 12

    c. 35 and 24

    d. 55 and 44

60. Students are given the following word problem: "A man begins driving west at an average speed of 45 miles per hour. After two and half hours, how far will he have driven?" Which equation should students devise to answer this question?

 a. 45 × 2.30
 b. 45 ÷ 2.30
 c. 45 ÷ 2.5
 d. 45 × 2.5

Questions 61-64: *Each sentence below has one or two blanks, each blank indicating that something has been omitted. For each question in this section, select the best answer from the choices provided.*

61. When they moved to a new apartment with much less storage room in the kitchen, they had to get rid of the _____ pots and pans.

 a. jaded
 b. tangential
 c. eclectic
 d. incongruous
 e. superfluous

62. The _____ that he used for death was so vague that people hearing it for the first time found it _____.

 a. enigma... pragmatic
 b. conjecture... astute
 c. erudition... circumspect
 d. euphemism... incoherent
 e. potentate... pedantic

63. Her _____ was seen by so many people and was so embarrassing to her that she became very _____ for the rest of the summer.

 a. veracity... sanctimonious
 b. chicanery... vituperative
 c. gaffe... reclusive
 d. altruism... laudatory
 e. effrontery... magnanimous

64. The realtor was _____ with calls about the new listing from the first day it was available.

 a. supplanted
 b. inundated
 c. disparaged
 d. castigated
 e. cajoled

Writing Skills and Knowledge

Questions 65-69: *The following sentences test correctness and effectiveness of expression. Part of each sentence or the entire sentence is underlined; beneath each sentence are four ways of phrasing the underlined material. Choice A repeats the original phrasing; the other* *three choices are different. For each question in this section, select the best answer from the choices given.*

65. The family, as a whole, are united against the sale of the land.
    a. The family, as a whole, are united
    b. The family, as a whole, is united
    c. As a whole, the family are united
    d. The family are united as a whole

66. Anyone on the girls' Junior Varsity Team was invited to put their name on the list to try out for the Varsity Team.
    a. was invited to put their name
    b. was invited to put her name
    c. is invited to put their name
    d. puts their name by invitation

67. All last summer, despite the sweltering heat and humidity, I wear a suit, tie and closed shoes for work.
    a. I wear a suit, tie and closed shoes for work.
    b. I nevertheless wear a suit, tie, and closed shoes for work.
    c. I wear a suit, a tie, and closed shoes for work.
    d. I wore a suit, tie and closed shoes for work.

68. People who like jazz don't usually turn into someone who likes country music.
    a. someone who likes country music
    b. someone who also likes country music
    c. people who like country music
    d. people who likes country music

69. We all are unique and each of us has our own way of solving problems.
    a. each of us has our own way
    b. each of us have our own way
    c. has our own way
    d. each have our own way

Question 70-73: *The following sentences test your ability to recognize grammar and usage errors. Each sentence contains either a single error or no error at all. No sentence contains more than one error. The error, if there is one, is lettered. If the sentence contains an error, select the one lettered part that must be changed to make the sentence correct. If the sentence is correct, select Choice E.*

70. The information that (a.) he was given by the two doctors (b.) make him realize how much his (c.) grandfather's health (d.) had declined. (e.) No error.

71. Quincy and his son Zane, (a.) neither of (b.) whom enjoy sporting events, (c.) is going to see a movie (d.) instead. (e.) No error.

72. The entire audience (a.) are rapt for the (b.) duration of the performance and applaud (c.) loudly when the (d.) curtain falls. (e.) No error.

73. (a.) <u>When asked about</u> her major job responsibilities, (b.) <u>Jodi answered that</u> she (c.) <u>responded to</u> client questions, conducted interviews, wrote reports, and (d.) <u>giving presentations</u>. (e.) <u>No error</u>.

Question 74-78: The following passage is an early draft of an essay. Some parts of the passage need to be rewritten. Read the passage and select the best answers for the questions that follow.

(1) Kids and people need to spend more time outside on a daily basis. <u>Last Child in the Woods: Saving Our Children from Nature-Deficit Disorder</u> is by Richard Louv and who says that in the last 30 years kids have become increasingly removed from nature to their detriment. **(2)** A 1991 study found that the radius children are allowed to roam outside their homes has shrunk to 1/9 of what it was 20 years before.

(3) Very bad for their physical fitness and mental health. **(4)** One in 5 American children is obese—compared with one in 20 in the late 1960s—and nearly 8 million kids suffer from mental illnesses, including depression and attention deficit disorder. **(5)** He says playing in nature helps reduce stress, increase concentration and promote problem-solving, this can help kids with attention deficit disorder and many other problems. Nature play can increase a child's self confidence and independence.

(6) Parents are scared to let kids play in the woods. **(7)** Parents are increasingly afraid of child abduction. **(8)** This is a terrible thing but actually very rare and fear of them should be balanced against the effect of fear on our daily lives.

(9) Kids play too many video games, watch too much television and are in the car for long stretches of time. **(10)** It is important to have the experience of wet feet and dirty hands and not just read about a frog, for example but to hold it in your hands.

(11) Parents and emphasize organized sports over imaginative play. **(12)** It's great that kids play so much organized sports now, but activity and physical play used to be what kids did with their free time, not twice a week for soccer practice.

74. Which version of the following portion of sentence 2 provides the most clarity? "*...is by Richard Louv and who says that in the last 30 years kids have become increasingly removed...*"
   a. is by Richard Louv and who says that in the last 30 years kids have become increasingly removed
   b. is by Richard Louv, who says that in the last 30 years kids have become increasingly removed
   c. is by Richard Louv and he says that in the last 30 years kids have become increasingly removed
   d. is by Richard Louv he says that in the last 30 years kids have become increasingly removed

75. Which of the following is the most succinct and clear way to re-write sentences 6 and 7?
    a. Parents are scared to let kids play in the woods. Parents are increasingly afraid of child abduction.
    b. Parents are scared to let kids play in the woods and are increasingly afraid of child abduction.
    c. Parents are scared to let kids play in the woods because they are increasingly afraid of child abduction.
    d. Parents are scared to let kids play in the woods so they are increasingly afraid of child abduction.

76. Which of the following represents the best version of sentence 3?
    a. Very bad for their physical fitness and mental health.
    b. It is very bad for their physical fitness and mental health.
    c. This is very bad for their physical fitness and mental health.
    d. This "Nature-Deficit Disorder" is very bad for their physical fitness and mental health.

77. Sentence 8 is poorly written. What can we infer the initial "This" of the sentence refers to?
    a. Parents
    b. Kids
    c. Play
    d. Child abduction

78. The paragraph that includes sentences 9 and 10 does not contain a clear point. Which of the following best describes what the author is likely trying to communicate in this paragraph?
    a. Nature is important.
    b. It is a problem that kids are increasingly entertained by technology, rather than by the sensory experience of nature.
    c. It is a problem that kids are increasingly lethargic.
    d. It is a problem that kids are removed from nature.

Application of Writing Skills and Knowledge to Classroom Instruction

Questions 79 and 80 are based on the following rough draft written by a student.
    My Trip to the Fire Station
    By Derek

    (1) Last week me and my class went to the fire station to look at the engines. (2) We was in the bus and going to the station when Ms. Glass said everybody needed to look out the window. (3) We heard the sirens and then as we got to the station a truck drove past with its lights going. (4) It was only one of the trucks at the station so we still got to do the tour just like we were supposed to. (5) One of the firemen let us try on his coat and it was real heavy. (6) It was a great trip for the class. (7) We also met the dog that lives at the station and we slid down the pole one at a time.

79. How should the student correct the first sentence?
   a. Eliminate the words me and.
   b. Substitute I for me.
   c. Eliminate the words to look at the engines.
   d. Place a comma after *week*.

80. Which sentence should be moved to a different place in the essay?
   a. 1
   b. 3
   c. 4
   d. 6

81. A student is composing a short persuasive essay about the importance of recycling. Which of the following would be the most effective thesis statement?
   a. "Recycling reduces waste and the consumption of natural resources."
   b. "People who don't recycle hate this planet."
   c. "Recycling is a fun way to make a difference."
   d. "I have recycled for my entire life."

82. A student writes the following sentence in a short story:
"We'll see what the commitee says," Darrell said to his sisters' friend.
The student has made an error of
   a. punctuation.
   b. grammar.
   c. spelling.
   d. diction.

83. Which of the following would be the best reference material for a fourth-grader's paper about space shuttles?
   a. scientific journal
   b. dictionary
   c. encyclopedia
   d. newspaper

84. A student's essay contains the following run-on sentence:
After playing baseball we went to the pool and we swam the water was cool.
Which of the following corrections is best?
   a. We played baseball, went to the pool, and swam, and the water was cool.
   b. After playing baseball, we went to the pool and swam in the cool water.
   c. We played baseball and swam in the pool's cool water.
   d. We played baseball, and then we went to the pool. We swam in the cool water.

85. A student's essay contains the following sentence:
After I watched the movie that afternoon, I spent the next week thinking about how to build a rocket.
What must the student do to correct this sentence?
    a. The initial clause should be written, "After I had watched the movie that afternoon."
    b. The comma should be eliminated.
    c. The phrase "the next week" should be moved to the end of the sentence.
    d. Nothing, the sentence is correct as written.

86. A student's essay contains the following sentence:
He claimed that he never went into the clubhouse with red paint.
The student has made an error of
    a. punctuation.
    b. spelling.
    c. grammar.
    d. diction.

87. Which word is NOT spelled correctly?
    a. nuisance
    b. prairie
    c. mysterious
    d. Wendesday

88. A student's essay contains the following sentence:
David Jackson, Jr., complained that the car had lost it's air-conditioning.
What must the student do to correct this sentence?
    a. Substitute lossed for lost.
    b. Eliminate the period after Jr.
    c. Eliminate the comma after Jr.
    d. Substitute *its* for *it's*

Questions 89 and 90 are based on the following rough draft written by a student.
    Setting Up a Tent
    By Darnell
    (1) I been campin a bunch of tims with my dad. (2) Wen you go campin you caint sit on the grond so yo gots to get a tent to slep in. (3) The best wons are mad of shiny materrl so the water caint get in. (4) First you gots to fine a flat plac to put yur tent in then you spreds it ot on the grend. (5) Yu puts in the pols and then it props up an you puts in the staks. (6) Wen you is don you can unzip it an get in an slep. (7) You better hav a sleping bag ur som blankets to slep in.

89. This essay suggests that the student needs remedial help with
    a. vocabulary.
    b. phonics.
    c. spelling.
    d. reading comprehension.

90. Which sentence would be the best thesis statement for this essay?
   a. 1
   b. 2
   c. 4
   d. 7

FREE Study Skills DVD Offer

Dear Customer,

Thank you for your purchase from Mometrix! We consider it an honor and privilege that you have purchased our product and want to ensure your satisfaction.

As a way of showing our appreciation and to help us better serve you, we have developed a Study Skills DVD that we would like to give you for <u>FREE</u>. **This DVD covers our "best practices" for studying for your exam, from using our study materials to preparing for the day of the test.**

All that we ask is that you email us your feedback that would describe your experience so far with our product. Good, bad or indifferent, we want to know what you think!

To get your **FREE Study Skills DVD**, email <u>freedvd@mometrix.com</u> with "FREE STUDY SKILLS DVD" in the subject line and the following information in the body of the email:

   a. The name of the product you purchased.

   b. Your product rating on a scale of 1-5, with 5 being the highest rating.

   c. Your feedback. It can be long, short, or anything in-between, just your impressions and experience so far with our product. Good feedback might include how our study material met your needs and will highlight features of the product that you found helpful.

   d. Your full name and shipping address where you would like us to send your free DVD.

If you have any questions or concerns, please don't hesitate to contact me directly.

Thanks again!

Sincerely,

Jay Willis
Vice President
<u>jay.willis@mometrix.com</u>
1-800-673-8175

Answers and Explanations

Reading Skills and Knowledge

1. D: Of the given options, only choice D can be inferred from the passage. The passage reads that parents should "try not to <u>feed into</u> oppositional behavior by reacting emotionally," which implies that reacting emotionally to defiant behavior can worsen it.

2. B: "ODD is a complex condition" is the best answer out of the four given. It is the only choice that can be inferred from the passage as a whole.

3. A: Oppositional means uncooperative.

4. B: is the best interpretation of paragraph one. The passage states that many people exhibit ODD symptoms from time to time.

5. B: <u>Feed into</u> in this sentence means to encourage oppositional behavior.

6. C: Someone with <u>low frustration tolerance</u> has a difficult time tolerating or dealing with frustration.

7. C: This passage is meant to inform the reader about ODD.

8. C: While some of these answer choices may contribute to ODD, the passage mentions only choice C, severe or unpredictable punishment.

9. A: The only statement directly supported by the passage is choice A.

10. C: The passage states that a pluralistic society means one that embraces "many points of view," which is closest in meaning to choice C, "tolerant."

11. B: This passage does not choose one point of view on the issue, so only choice B is in keeping with the passage's purpose, which is to explain the disagreements between the earliest political parties in the US.

12. B: The word <u>competitive</u> means that the country would be able to compete financially with other countries. Choice B, stronger, is the best choice.

13. B: The passage explains the conflicting interests these two political parties represent.

14. A: <u>It</u> refers to the noun "identity." Choice A is the best choice.

15. B: Since the passage does not choose to argue a particular point of view, the best choice would be the most neutral statement, choice B.

16. D: Best reflects the true position of the Federalist Party.

17. A: Best represents the Democratic-Republican Party's perspective.

18. B: The final paragraph mentions the Civil War only to show that these differing perspectives would not be easily reconciled. Choice B is the best answer.

Application of Reading Skills and Knowledge to Classroom Instruction

19. A: Jason comments on the time in which the masterpieces were painted. B is incorrect because the contents of the paintings are not described. C is incorrect because he does not mention the artists. D is incorrect because the architecture of the Uffizi Gallery is not mentioned.

20. B: Students could recognize the signal words. A is incorrect because defining historical events would not help recognition of comparison and contrast or cause and effect. C is incorrect since a timeline would not help recognition of comparison and contrast or cause and effect. D is incorrect since maps would not help recognition of comparison and contrast or cause and effect.

21. C: The titles are in chronological order. A is incorrect because the titles do not show comparison and contrast. B is incorrect because the titles do not show cause and effect. D is incorrect because the titles do not show problem and solution.

22. D: Hidden message techniques have increased through the years. A is incorrect because hidden message techniques have not remained the same through the years. B is incorrect because hidden message techniques have not decreased through the years. C is incorrect because hidden message techniques have not decreased in importance.

23. C: The teacher is involving them in the concept of faith through Bonhoeffer's life. A is incorrect because details of World War II are not discussed.
B is incorrect because details of Germany are not discussed. D is incorrect because the teacher is not primarily providing a multicultural true story.

24. A: The passage is colloquial. B is incorrect because the passage is not abstract. C is incorrect because the passage is not formal. D is incorrect because the passage is not allusive.

25. D: It is the complete answer. A is incorrect because it is only a partial answer. B is incorrect because it is only a partial answer. C is incorrect because it is only a partial answer.

26. B: The author indicated that she revised her books. A is incorrect because the author indicated that revisions were always necessary in her books. C is incorrect because the author did not suggest that revisions showed an inability to write a piece initially. D is incorrect because the author would not have revised her work if it had not improved it.

27. A: This brief paragraph will encourage students to use writing as a means for personal exploration and self-expression. B is incorrect because this writing assignment is not a mandate to disagree with others. C is incorrect because the structure of the novel is not shown in the passage. D is incorrect because the plot of the novel is not shown in the passage.

28. B: This is use of parallel construction. A is incorrect because this is not use of alliteration. C is incorrect because this is not use of metaphors. D is incorrect because this is not use of similes.

29. C: It shows his interest in codebreaking. A is incorrect because it is not his interest in plotting. B is incorrect because it is not his interest in conflict. D is incorrect because it does not show his interest in characterization.

30. D: Rewriting significantly and giving attribution to research sources will avoid plagiarism. A is incorrect because rewriting significantly is only part of the answer. B is incorrect because giving attribution to the sources is only part of the answer. C is incorrect because copying word-for-word without attribution is plagiarism and would not be advised.

Mathematics Skills and Knowledge

31. A: An odd number can be considered as an even number N plus 1. Two even numbers added together produce an even number, so the result of adding an odd and an even number must be an even number plus 1, which is odd. For example, $4 + 3 = 7$.

32. D: In scientific notation, the exponent indicates the number of places that the decimal must be moved to the right. For example, $2.3 \times 10^1 = 2.1 \times 10 = 21$. Moving the decimal three places to the right in this problem is equivalent to multiplying by 1,000, so the result is 6,190.

33. B: The perimeter of a square is 4 times the length of a side. Therefore, in this case, the side s must equal $s = \dfrac{16}{4} = 4$. The area A is found by squaring the length a, or $A = s^2 = 4^2 = 16$. Since the area is 16 ft², choice B is correct.

34. C: The square root of a number which is raised to the 4th power is the same number raised to the 2nd power. That is, $\sqrt{2^4} = 2^2 = 4$. Since 4 x 4 = 16, C is correct.

35. B: The average, or arithmetic mean, is computed by totaling all the measurements and dividing by the number of measurements. Let T_B represent the sum of the heights of the boys in the class, and T_G the sum of the heights of the girls. If N is the number of students in the class, there are $N/2$ boys and $N/2$ girls. The average height of the boys is then $\dfrac{T_B}{\frac{N}{2}} = \dfrac{2T_B}{N} = 62$. Similarly, the average height of the girls is $\dfrac{2T_G}{N}$. The average height of all

the students is equal to $\frac{T_B + T_G}{N} = \frac{T_B}{N} + \frac{T_G}{N} = 60$. Therefore, $\frac{T_G}{N} = 60 - \frac{T_B}{N} = 60 - 31 = 29$, and the average height for the girls is 2 x 29 = 58.

36. C: The area of a circle is equal to πr², where r is the radius. Therefore, $\pi r^2 = 36\pi$, and $r = \sqrt{36} = 6$. Since the diameter is two times the radius, it is equal to 12.

37. C: Each throw of the dart is an independent event, and has no influence on the outcome of any other throw. Every time the dart is thrown, it has a 50% chance of landing on black, irrespective of the results of previous throws.

38. D: The integers are -4, -3, -2, -1, 0, +1, +2, +3, +4, +5, and +6.

39. B: The verbal description "five times a number m squared" means that m must be squared, and the resulting number multiplied by 5. Choice C is incorrect because the value within the parentheses is evaluated first, so that both 5 and m are squared. This results in a value of $25m^2$, which is incorrect.

40. C: The area scales with the square of the radius, so if the radius increases in length by a factor of 2, the area will increase by 2², or 4. Since $Area = \pi r^2$, if the radius r is replaced with 2r, this yields $Area = \pi(2r)^2 = 4\pi r^2$, which is 4 times the original area.

41. C: Since 11 – 5 = 6, then 3x = 6, and $x = \frac{6}{3} = 2$.

42. A: To answer this question, we first determine the total cost of the onions and carrots, since these prices are given. This will equal (2 x $3.69 + 3 x $4.29) = $20.25. Next, this sum is subtracted from the total cost of the vegetables to determine the cost of the mushrooms: $24.15 - $20.25 = $3.90. Finally, the cost of the mushrooms is divided by the quantity in lbs to determine the cost per lb:
Cost per lb $= \frac{\$3.90}{1.5} = \$2.60$

43. D: Adding a constant to each side of the inequality does not change the sense of the inequality, so begin by adding 12: $4x < 4 + 12$, or $4x < 16$. Dividing each side of an inequality by a positive number does not change the sense of the inequality either, so now divide both sides by 4 in order to isolate the variable, x: $x < \frac{16}{4}$, or $x < 4$.

44. D: First, compute the value enclosed by the parentheses, $3b + 5 = 3 \times 7 + 5 = 26$. Next, compute 4$a$ = -24. Note that a is negative, so that this product is negative as well. The product $4a(3b + 5)$ will therefore be negative as well, and equals -624. Finally, add the value of 2b, or 2 x 7 =14, to -624, to get the final answer - $624 + 14 = -610$.

45. B: Since the rate, miles per minute, is constant, this can be solved by setting up a proportion: $\frac{miles}{min} = \frac{10}{12} = \frac{210}{t}$. Now, solve for $t = \frac{210 \times 12}{10} = 252$ minutes. Finally, convert

- 26 -

to hours by dividing this total by 60, since there are 60 minutes in an hour: $t = \dfrac{252}{60} = 4$ hours and 12 minutes.

46. C: Define a variable t as the elapsed time in minutes from the time the first airplane takes off. Then at any time the distance traveled by the first plane is $d_1 = 250t$. The second plane takes off 30 minutes later, so at any time the distance that it has traveled is $d_2 = 280(t-30)$. This plane will overtake the first when the two distances are equal, that is when $d_1 = d_2$, or when $250t = 280(t-30)$. Solve this last equation for t. First use the distributive property: $250t = 280t - 30 \times 280 = 280t - 8{,}400$.
Next, add 8,400 to each side of the equation: $250t + 8{,}400 = 280t$.
Next, subtract $250t$ from each side of the equation: $8{,}400 = 30t$.
Next, divide both sides by 30: $280 = t$.
This gives the value of t in minutes. Convert to hours by dividing 280 by 60 minutes per hour, which yields an elapsed time of 4 hours and 40 minutes. Since the first plane left at 2 PM, 4 hours and 40 minutes later is 6:40 PM.

47. A: This equation represents a linear relationship of slope 3.60 that passes through the origin, or zero point. The table shows that for each hour of rental, the cost increases by an amount equal to $3.60. This corresponds to the slope of the equation. Of course, if the bicycle is not rented at all (0 hours) there will be no charge ($0), so the line must pass through the origin. Relationship A is the only one that satisfies these criteria.

48. A: Besides the $600 he has remaining; Chan has paid out a total of 85% (30% + 30% +25%) of his bonus for the expenses described in the question. Therefore, the $600 represents the remaining 15%. Remember that 15% can be written as 15/100. To determine his total bonus, solve $\dfrac{15}{100}x = 600$. So, $x = \dfrac{100}{15} \times 600 = 4{,}000$ dollars.

Application of Mathematics Skills and Knowledge of Classroom Instruction

49. A: The first operation to be performed is multiplying five by four and three. This question requires knowledge of the order of operations, or the sequence in which arithmetic functions should be performed in a complex number sentence. The order of operations is parentheses, exponents, multiplication, addition, and subtraction. In this problem, the first step is to resolve the parenthetical expression. This can be done either by multiplying five by four and three and then multiplying the products, or by multiplying four and three and then multiplying this product by five.

50. C: The equation $P = a + b + c + d$ suggests the necessary calculation for this problem. Perimeter is found by adding the lengths of the sides together. Since the four sides of this shape are known to have varying lengths, they must be represented by four different variables. If the shape was a rectangle (that is, if it had two sets of two equal sides), answer choice D could be correct.

51. C: When a student gives the answer "ten two," he is probably referring to 10:10. Students who are learning to read an analog clock will often confuse hours with minutes. A student who gives the minutes as "two" most likely sees the minute hand over the two, which actually indicates ten minutes past the hour.

52. B: The student's answer is incorrect because baking trays cannot be subdivided. In other words, a baking tray only comes in units of one, so the man in the word problem will need seven trays. The last tray will be filled only one quarter of the way full. This problem underscores the necessity of reading comprehension when solving word problems. Students should not just translate the terms of the word problem into the language of math. They must also check to make sure their method and solution is logical.

53. A: The student could use $(3 \times 75) \div 5$ to solve this problem. Answer choice A could be expressed $3/5 \times 75/1$, which simplifies to $(3 \times 75)/5 = 225/5 = 45$. The answer then is that $3/5$ of 75 is 45.

54. D: The student's answer is incorrect, most likely because she has added rather than subtracted five to both sides. When solving a simple algebraic equation of this type, the goal is to isolate the variable on one side. This is done by eliminating the other terms and coefficients one by one. The most common first step in this problem would be to eliminate the 5 by subtracting an equal amount from both sides of the equation. This would leave $2x = 15$, which leads to the correct solution $x = 7.5$. If five was added, however, the resulting equation would be $2x = 25$, which would lead to the student's incorrect answer.

55. C: The number sentence should be written $4(3 + 7) \div 8$. The student erred by placing a multiplication symbol in between the three and seven. The problem states that the sum of the products of four and three and four and seven is to be divided by eight. In other words, four must be multiplied by both three and seven, with the resulting products added together. One way to express this is $4(3 + 7)$. Another would be $4 \times 3 + 4 \times 7$.

56. A: The first step in this operation must be finding the lowest common denominator. Fractions may not be added together or subtracted from one another unless they have the same denominator. The lowest common denominator is found by listing the multiples of the denominators until a common multiple is found. In this case, the lists would proceed as 8, 16, 24 and 6, 12, 18, 24, indicating that the lowest common denominator is 24. To convert $3/8$ into a fraction with a denominator of 24, numerator and denominator must be multiplied by 3: $3/8 \times 3/3 = 9/24$. To convert $5/6$ into a fraction with a denominator of 24, both numerator and denominator must be multiplied by 4: $5/6 \times 4/4 = 20/24$. With common denominators, then, the problem can now be solved: $9/24 + 20/24 = 29/24$, or $1 \frac{5}{24}$.

57. A: The student's list is correct and comprehensive: it contains all of the factors of 32. The factors of a number are all of those whole numbers that can be divided evenly into the given number. Another way of expressing this is that the factors of a number are all of the terms that can be used in a two-term multiplication problem that produces the given number. The following multiplication problems produce 32: 32×1, 16×2, and 8×4. These are the factors of 32.

58. A: Students could use the equation (5 × 4) ÷ 2 = ? to solve this problem. There are five teams, each of which will play for others. This accounts for the 5 × 4. However, each game includes two teams, so the product must be divided by two. Otherwise, the student would be counting Team A's game against Team B as well as Team B's game against Team A. Another equation that could be used to solve this problem is 4 + 3 + 2 + 1 = ? In this equation, the first term represents the number of games played by Team A, the second term the games played by Team B except the game against Team A, the third term the games played by Team C except the games against Teams A and B, and the final term the games played by Team D except those against Teams A, B, and C. Team E does not need to be included in this equation because all of its games have been counted. However the problem is solved, the answer is 10.

59. C: 35 and 24 should not be on this list because they do not have a ratio of 5:4. Indeed, the ratio of 35 to 24 cannot be simplified. Pairs of numbers will only have the correct ratio if they can be produced by multiplying five and four by the same numbers. For instance, 25 and 20 are produced by multiplying five and four by five. 55 and 44 are produced by multiplying five and four by eleven.

60. D: Students should use the equation 45 × 2.5 to answer this question. The answer is 112.5 miles.

Writing Skills and Knowledge

61. E: The blank in this sentence should be a word that describes items one would get rid of if one had to (here, because of space concerns). Superfluous is the best fit because it indicates that the items being gotten rid of are extra and perhaps unnecessary for that reason.

62. D: The only choice in which the first word of the pair fits the context of the sentence is (D), so all other choices can be eliminated.

63. C: The first blank in this sentence needs to be something that would be embarrassing to the subject of the sentence. Chicanery, gaffe, and effrontery meet this requirement. Of those three choices, choice (C) has the second word, reclusive, that most compellingly describes a potential behavior or reaction someone might exhibit after being publicly embarrassed.

64. B: The blank in this sentence needs to describe something that the calls did to the realtor. The only word that fits this need is inundated. The agent was inundated, or swamped, with calls.

65. B: The word "family" is singular. The verb thus needs to be the singular "is," rather than the plural "are."

66. B: The word "anyone" is singular, so the phrasing "their name" is incorrect.

67. D: "All last summer" indicates a time in the past, so the present tense form of "to wear" is incorrect.

68. C: The word "people" is plural, and is incorrectly matched with the singular word "someone."

69. A: Sentence is correct.

70. B: The verb tense is incorrect. It should be "made" rather than "make."

71. C: The verb "is" is singular, and does not agree with the plural subject "Quincy and his son Zane." The verb should be "are" instead.

72. A: A collective noun, "the audience" is singular, and takes singular verbs. Therefore, "are" is incorrect, and should be "is."

73. D: The verb "giving" is in the wrong form. It should be "gave."

74. B: The part of the sentence "who says that..." is a parenthetical phrase about Richard Louv, not about the subject of the sentence. The "and who" is therefore incorrect, and the phrase needs to be set off from the sentence by a comma.

75. C: The best answer is (C) because it best captures the logical connection of the sentences: the fear of abduction is the *reason* parents are afraid to let kids play in the woods.

76. D: The sentence needs a subject. Answer (D) is the one that most clearly identifies a subject.

77. D: The "this" logically must refer to child abduction. Although not stated explicitly, it is the only choice that could logically be described as "a terrible thing" and "very rare."

78. B: Although the paragraph does not make its point explicitly, it clearly states that kids are spending too much time with video games and TV (being entertained by technology) and would be helped by more time getting their feet and hands dirty and touching things rather than just reading about them (having a +sensory experience of nature).

Application of Writing Skills and Knowledge to Classroom Instruction

79. A: The student should correct the first sentence by eliminating the words *me and*. Since the student has said that his class went to the fire station, it may be assumed that he went as well. Substituting *I* for *me* would be more grammatically correct, but no less redundant. The other answer choices describe unnecessary changes.

80. D: The sentence "It was a great trip for the class" should be moved to a different place in the essay. This sentence would be an appropriate final statement for the essay. Up until this point, the student has proceeded in chronological order through the events of the day. Sentence 6 breaks this trend to make a more general statement about the field trip. This statement would be more appropriate at the end of the essay.

81. A: The most effective thesis statement would be "Recycling reduces waste and the consumption of natural resources." A thesis statement expresses the main idea of the essay. Any of the answer choices could serve as a thesis statement, depending on the rest of the essay. However, since the question specifies that the assignment is a short persuasive essay, the effectiveness of the other answer choices becomes dubious. Answer choice B is a personal attack, hardly the most effective strategy for persuasion. Answer choice C focuses on the pleasure of recycling, which is not as relevant to its importance as the facts in answer choice A. Answer choice D is an autobiographical statement that has no real bearing on the importance of recycling, and would not be persuasive to a reader.

82. C: The student has made an error of spelling. The correct spelling is *committee*. This sentence contains other details that look questionable but that cannot be called errors out of context. The comma should be placed inside the final quotation mark, and the apostrophe is in the correct place assuming that the author is referring to the friend of more than one of Darrell's sisters.

83. C: An encyclopedia would be the best reference material for a fourth-grader's paper about space shuttles. When answering a question of this type, it is important to note the grade of the student. A fourth-grader is not likely to understand the content of a scientific journal, even though this source may provide the most detailed information about space shuttles. A dictionary merely provides definitions and etymologies, and would not contain sufficient information for an entire paper. A newspaper might reference space shuttles as they figure in current events, but it would not have basic background information on this type of subject.

84. B: The best correction of the student's run-on sentence is "After playing baseball, we went to the pool and swam in the cool water." The other answer choices are grammatically correct, but each of them is weak in another way. Answer choice A has a boring structure, and it is jarring to the reader to introduce a new subject (the water) in the last clause. Answer choice C doesn't clearly indicate the sequence of events, and contains an awkward phrase (*pool's cool*). Answer choice D is choppy and divides the subject matter in an odd way. It makes more sense to group in one sentence the ideas related to swimming.

85. A: To correct this sentence, the student must write the initial clause as "After I had watched the movie that afternoon." This sentence describes two actions that took place in the past. To establish the sequence in which they happened, the student must put the dependent clause in the past perfect tense (had watched) and the independent clause in the past tense. This shows that the student watched the movie before thinking about how to build a rocket.

86. C: The student has made an error of grammar. The placement of the modifying phrase "with red paint" makes it impossible to tell whether the person or the clubhouse had the red paint. If the person had the paint, the sentence could be written as follows: He claimed that he never went with red paint into the clubhouse. If the paint is on the clubhouse, the sentence could be written like this: He claimed that he never went into the clubhouse, which was painted red.

87. D: *Wendesday* is not spelled correctly. The correct spelling is *Wednesday*. This word has an unusual spelling, as the *d* does not sound as if it should come before the *n*. A

paraprofessional needs to develop an ability to judge spelling at a glance, so that corrections can be made while students are still working on a draft.

88. D: To correct this sentence, the student must substitute *its* for *it's*. The student has used the contraction for *it is* rather than the possessive form of *it*. The student's handling of *Jr.* is correct. When this title is abbreviated, it should be followed by a period even in the middle of a sentence. Also, it is acceptable to set aside this abbreviation with commas, though this is not mandatory.

89. C: This essay suggests that the student needs remedial help with spelling. The essay makes sense, and the student demonstrates sufficient vocabulary to make his point. However, the spelling in this essay is poor. Nevertheless, the spelling errors do not betray a lack of phonics knowledge; indeed, the student's misspellings seem to be the product of simply sounding words out rather than having a solid grasp of English spelling.

90. B: The second sentence of this essay would be the best thesis statement. The title of the essay is "Setting Up a Tent," and the second sentence provides the most general statement of this theme. Of course, none of the sentences in this essay really serves as an effective thesis. The first sentence somewhat introduces the subject of camping but is basically irrelevant to the rest of the essay.

Practice Test #2

Practice Questions

Reading Skills and Knowledge

Questions 1-8 pertain to the following passage:

It is tempting to think that your eyes are simply mirrors that reflect whatever is in front of them. Researchers, however, have shown that your brain is constantly working to create the impression of a continuous, uninterrupted world.

For instance, in the last ten minutes, you have blinked your eyes around 200 times. You have probably not been aware of any of these interruptions in your visual world. Something you probably have not seen in a long time without the aid of a mirror is your nose. It is always right there, down in the bottom corner of your vision, but your brain filters it out so that you are not aware of your nose unless you purposefully look at it.

Nor are you aware of the artery that runs right down the middle of your retina. It creates a large blind spot in your visual field, but you never notice the hole it leaves. To see this blind spot, try the following: Cover your left eye with your hand. With your right eye, look at the O on the left. As you move your head closer to the O, the X will disappear as it enters the blind spot caused by your optical nerve.

O   X

Your brain works hard to make the world look continuous!

1. The word <u>filters</u>, as used in this passage, most nearly means:
    a. Alternates
    b. Reverses
    c. Ignores
    d. Depends

2. The word <u>retina</u>, as used in this passage, most nearly means:
    a. Optical illusion
    b. Part of the eye
    c. Pattern
    d. Blindness

3. Which of the following statements can be inferred from this passage?
    a. Not all animals' brains filter out information.
    b. Visual perception is not a passive process.
    c. Blind spots cause accidents.
    d. The eyes never reflect reality.

4. What is the author's purpose for including the two letters in the middle of the passage?
   a. To demonstrate the blind spot in the visual field.
   b. To organize the passage.
   c. To transition between the last two paragraphs of the passage.
   d. To prove that the blind spot is not real.

5. What is the main purpose of this passage?
   a. To persuade the reader to pay close attention to blind spots.
   b. To explain the way visual perception works.
   c. To persuade the reader to consult an optometrist if the O and X disappear.
   d. To prove that vision is a passive process.

6. Based on the passage, which of the following statements is true?
   a. The brain cannot accurately reflect reality.
   b. Glasses correct the blind spot caused by the optical nerve.
   c, Vision is the least important sense.
   d. The brain fills in gaps in the visual field.

7. The author mentions the nose to illustrate what point?
   a. The brain filters out some visual information.
   b. Not all senses work the same way.
   c. Perception is a passive process.
   d. The sense of smell filters out information.

8. Which of the following statements can be inferred from the second paragraph?
   a. The brain filters out the sound created by the shape of the ears.
   b. The brain does not perceive all activity in the visual field.
   c. Closing one eye affects depth perception.
   d. The brain evolved as a result of environmental factors.

Questions 9-16 pertain to the following passage:

Easily the most recognizable constellation in the night sky, the Big Dipper has captured the imaginations of people of every culture and every historical period. Not all people have seen the shape of a dipper, though. In fact, the Big Dipper is only part of a larger constellation called Ursa Major. The seven stars that make up the handle and pan of the Big Dipper are just a few of the eighteen stars that make up Ursa Major, a name the Greeks gave the constellation that means "The Great Bear."

Native Americans also saw the constellation as a bear, but they saw the bear in the cup of the dipper. Some Native American groups saw the stars of the handle as three warriors hunting the bear; others saw them as three cubs following their mother. In England the cluster of stars is thought to resemble a plow, but in Scandinavia it is known as a wagon. In ancient Mayan astronomy, it was called a spoon. Arabic astronomers saw the bowl as a coffin and the three stars in the handle as mourners at a funeral. Others have seen it as a bull's thigh, or even a governmental organization.

American slaves sang a song called "Follow the Drinking Gourd." On one level, the song sounded like it was about the cup the slaves used to drink

- 34 -

water, but it also worked as a <u>code</u> to teach slaves who wanted their freedom to escape to the north by following the Big Dipper when traveling by night.

The Big Dipper is <u>circumpolar</u>, so it can be seen all night long. This reason may account in part for its easy visibility among the constellations.

9. As used in the passage, the word "circumpolar" most nearly means:
   a. Seasonal
   b. Stays in the sky all night
   c. Stationary
   d. Bright

10. Which statement best describes the author's purpose in writing this passage?
   a. To present correct and incorrect interpretations of the Big Dipper.
   b. To explain the secret codes of American slaves.
   c. To persuade the reader to spend more time viewing the night skies.
   d. To inform the reader of different interpretations of the Big Dipper.

11. Which statement can be inferred from the third paragraph?
   a. Stars can be used to navigate unknown areas.
   b. Slavery was an immoral institution.
   c. All old spirituals contain secret messages.
   d. Slaves adopted the Native American interpretation of the Big Dipper.

12. Which of the following statements is true of the Native American interpretation of the Big Dipper?
   a. The handle was interpreted as mourners at a funeral.
   b. Their interpretation was inherited from the Mayan civilization.
   c. Some groups interpreted the three stars of the handle differently.
   d, They also used the stars to navigate their way to freedom from slavery.

13. Which of the following statements seems true based on the passage?
   a. No two cultures share the same interpretation of the Big Dipper.
   b. Navigating by the stars has largely been replaced by technology.
   c. The stars have inspired the imaginations of many cultures.
   d. Myths are often based in truth.

14. According to the passage, the word "code" most nearly means:
   a. Cipher
   b. Interpretation
   c. Secret message
   d. Slang

15. According to the passage, which one of the following statements is true of the constellations?
   a. Seen from another galaxy, constellations would not appear the same.
   b. Some stars are closer to the Earth than others.
   c. The light from some stars takes billions of years to arrive on the Earth.
   d. Many different cultures are compelled to connect individual stars to others and form constellations.

16. Which of the following statements best captures the meaning of the final paragraph?
   a. The Big Dipper is can be difficult to recognize.
   b. The Big Dipper is easy to see because it stays in the sky all night long.
   c. The Big Dipper is special because it is not always easy to see.
   d. The Big Dipper is easy to see because it contains the brightest stars in the night sky.

17. *Beowulf* is an epic poem that is important because it is often viewed as the first significant work of English literature. Although it was first written in 700A.D., it is thought to be even hundreds of years older than that. It is believed that the story of *Beowulf* was told for centuries before it ever made its way on to paper. It is still taught today in various schools and universities.
Beowulf is a significant poem because
   a. it was first written down in 700A.D.
   b. it was told for centuries before it was written down.
   c. it is still taught today in academic settings.
   d. it is the first important work of English literature.

18. At one time, people who wanted to be writers had to write a query letter to a magazine and then wait weeks, sometimes months, for a response, which was usually a rejection. Today, with blogs, virtually anybody can put their work out there for others to view. It's as easy as setting up your blog, naming it, and posting anything you want: opinions, poems, short stories, news articles, etc. Of course, while people who have blogs may choose to call themselves writers or journalists, it's unlikely they are making a living by putting their random thoughts out there into cyberspace.
It can be concluded that:
   a. it is easier to make a living as a writer now.
   b. there are more people who want to be writers now.
   c. most people do not submit query letters to magazines anymore.
   d. there is no approval process for getting a blog.

Application of Reading Skills and Knowledge to Classroom Instruction

19. A teacher is working with a group of third graders at the same reading level. Her goal is to improve reading fluency. She asks each child in turn to read a page from a book about mammal young. She asks the children to read with expression. She also reminds them they don't need to stop between each word; they should read as quickly as they comfortably can. She cautions them, however, not to read so quickly that they leave out or misread a word. The teacher knows the components of reading fluency are:
    a. Speed, drama, and comprehension
    b. Cohesion, rate, and prosody
    c. Understanding, rate, and prosody
    d. Rate, accuracy, and prosody

20. A third-grade teacher has several students reading above grade level. Most of the remaining students are reading at grade level. There are also a few students reading below grade level. She decides to experiment. Her hypothesis is that by giving the entire class a chapter book above grade level, high-level readers will be satisfied, grade-level readers will be challenged in a positive way, and students reading below grade level will be inspired to improve. Her method is most likely to:
    a. Succeed, producing students reading at an Instructional reading level. High-level readers will be happy to be given material appropriate to their reading level. Grade-level readers will challenge themselves to improve reading strategies in order to master the text. Because only a few of the students are reading below grade level, the other students, who feel happy and energized, will inspire the slower readers by modeling success.
    b. Succeed, producing students reading at an Independent reading level. High-level readers will independently help grade-level readers who will, in turn, independently help those below grade level.
    c. Fail, producing students at a Frustration reading level. Those reading below grade level are likely to give up entirely. Those reading at grade level are likely to get frustrated and form habits that will actually slow down their development.
    d. Fail, producing students reading at a Chaotic reading level. By nature, children are highly competitive. The teacher has not taken into consideration multiple learning styles. The children who are at grade level will either become bitter and angry at those whose reading level is above grade level or simply give up. The children reading below grade level will not be able to keep up and will in all likelihood act out their frustration or completely shut down.

21. Of the three tiers of words, the most important words for direct instruction are:
    a. Tier-one words
    b. Common words
    c. Tier-two words
    d. Words with Latin roots

22. At the beginning of each month, Mr. Yi has Jade read a page or two from a book she hasn't seen before. He notes the total number of words in the section, and also notes the number of times she leaves out or misreads a word. If Jade reads the passage with less than 3% error, Mr. Yi is satisfied that Jade is:
   a. Reading with full comprehension.
   b. Probably bored and should try a more difficult book.
   c. Reading at her Independent reading level.
   d. Comfortable with the syntactical meaning.

23. The purpose of corrective feedback is:
   a. To provide students with methods for explaining to the teacher or classmates what a passage was about.
   b. To correct an error in reading a student has made, specifically clarifying where and how the error was made so that the student can avoid similar errors in the future.
   c. To provide a mental framework that will help the student correctly organize new information.
   d. To remind students that error is essential in order to truly understand and that it is not something to be ashamed of.

24. Dr. Jenks is working with a group of high school students. They are about to read a science book about fossils. Before they begin, she writes the words *stromatolites, fossiliferous,* and *eocene* on the board. She explains the meaning of each word. These words are examples of:
   a. Academic words
   b. Alliteration
   c. Content-specific words
   d. Ionization

25. Which of the following best explains the importance prior knowledge brings to the act of reading?
   a. Prior knowledge is information the student gets through researching a topic prior to reading the text. A student who is well-prepared through such research is better able to decode a text and retain its meaning.
   b. Prior knowledge is knowledge the student brings from previous life or learning experiences to the act of reading. It is not possible for a student to fully comprehend new knowledge without first integrating it with prior knowledge.
   c. Prior knowledge is predictive. It motivates the student to look for contextual clues in the reading and predict what is likely to happen next.
   d. Prior knowledge is not important to any degree to the act of reading, because every text is self-contained and therefore seamless. Prior knowledge is irrelevant in this application.

26. A reading teacher is assessing an eighth grader to determine her reading level. Timed at a minute, the student reads with 93% accuracy. She misreads an average of seven words out of 100. What is her reading level?
   a. She is reading at a Frustration level.
   b. She is reading at an Excellence level.
   c. She is reading at an Instructional level.
   d. She is reading at an Independent level.

For question 27 read the following story, then answer the question that follows.

The kindergarten teacher is concerned about three of her students. While they are enthusiastic about writing, they do not always recognize letters, confusing b, d, and p, or e and o. They do, however, know which sounds go with certain letters when they are orally drilled. When they write, they appear to be attempting letter–sound associations.

"Now I'm writing *M*," the teacher heard one boy say as he scripted a large *N* in the upper right corner of his paper. He studied it for a moment and added, "Nope, it needs another leg." The student then wrote an *I* beside the *N*. "There," he said. "Now you are an *M*. I can write the word, 'man,' because now I have *M*." The child then moved to the lower left corner of the paper. "M-A-N," he said to himself, slowly pronouncing each sound. "I already have that *M*. Here is where the rest of the word goes." He turned the paper sideways and wrote *N*.

The second child sang to herself as she gripped the crayon and scribbled lines here and there on her paper. Some of the lines resembled letters, but few actually were. Others were scribbles. As she "wrote," she seemed to be making up a story and seemed to believe she was writing the story down. The third child didn't vocalize at all while he worked. He gripped the paper and carefully wrote the same letter over and over and over. Sometimes the letter was large, sometimes tiny. He turned the paper in every direction so that sometimes the letter was sideways or upside down. Sometimes he flipped it backward. "What are you writing?" the teacher asked him. "My name," the child told her. The teacher then realized the letter was, indeed, the first letter of his name. She gently told him he had done a fine job of writing the first letter of his name. Did he want her to help him write the rest of it? "Nope," he cheerfully told her, "it's all here." He pointed at one of the letters and "read" his full name. He pointed at another letter and again seemed to believe it represented all the sounds of his name.

27. The kindergarten teacher isn't certain if these children are exhibiting signs of a reading disability or other special needs. What should the teacher do?

    a. Nothing. These children are simply at an early stage in the reading/writing process.

    b. Nothing. She doesn't want to have to tell the parents that their children are sub-par in terms of intelligence. They are perfectly nice children and can contribute to society in other ways. She resolves to give them extra attention in other areas to help them build confidence.

    c. She should recommend that the parents take the children to be tested for a number of reading disorders, including dyslexia.

    d. She should arrange a meeting between herself, the school psychologist, and the reading specialist to discuss the matter and resolve it using a three-pronged approach.

28. Using brain imaging, researchers have discovered that dyslexic readers use the
_____ side(s) of their brains, while non-dyslexic readers use the _____ side(s)
of their brains.
   a. Left; right
   b. Right; left
   c. Right and left; left
   d. Right; left and right

29. A high school class reads an essay about the possible effects of sexual activity on teens.
The author's position is very clear: She believes young people should avoid sex because
they aren't mature enough to take the necessary steps to remain safe. The author cites facts,
research studies, and statistics to strengthen her position. This type of writing is called:
   a. Expository
   b. Narrative
   c. Persuasive
   d. Didactic

30. The second graders are confused. They've learned to hear and count syllables. They
understand that contractions such as *won't*, *didn't*, and *we're* represent two words
converted into one. Now the teacher is trying to explain compound words. She has shown
the children that a compound word is made of two words and has a meaning that is a little
different from either of words that compose it. She pronounces *doghouse*, and asks if it is
one word or two. "Two," the students correctly respond. The teacher now says *parent*.
Again, the students tell her it's two words. The teacher explains there are two syllables but
not two words. One child nods and says, "Like the word 'didn't.' That's two words but it
sounds like one." What is the best way for the teacher to correct the students'
misunderstanding?
   a. Point out compound words the children use throughout the day. Write them on the
   board, and ask students to list them in their writing journals.
   b. Assess the degree of confusion. Give the students a quiz listing a number of two-
   syllable words, compound words, and contractions. Ask the students to cross out the
   two-syllable words and contractions.
   c. Write a compound word such as doghouse on the board. Underline dog, and then
   house. Beneath the words draw a picture of a dog and a house, joined with a plus sign.
   Next, write another compound word and ask the class to draw the pictures in their
   journals. Give the students a handout with several compound words. Ask them to
   underline the two words, then to draw the pictures.
   d. Turn the lesson into fun by suggesting the students invent new compound words.
   Demonstrate by inventing one such as nosemitten instead of scarf. Children learn more
   readily when they are enjoying it.

Mathematics Skills and Knowledge

31. In 1999, an office supply store sold 14,000 pens. In 2009, it sold only 12,600 pens. By
what percent did the store's pen sales decrease from 1999 to 2009?
   a. 1%
   b. 5%
   c. 10%
   d. 15%

32. 30% of 50 equals 50% of what number?
    a. 30
    b. 25
    c. 20
    d. 15

33. If the average of 7 and x is equal to the average of 9, 4, and x, what is the value of x?
    a. 4
    b. 5
    c. 6
    d. 7

34. If four friends had an average score of 92 on a test, what was Annie's score if Bill got an 86, Clive got a 98 and Demetrius got a 90?
    a. 88
    b. 90
    c. 92
    d. 94

35. If $3x - 2 = 1$, then $x =$
    a. 4
    b. 3
    c. 2
    d. 1

36. If a restaurant's salad dressing is made of a ratio of ¾ cup oil to ¼ cup vinegar, how many cups of vinegar are there in 6 cups of salad dressing?
    a. ½
    b. 1 ½
    c. 1 ¾
    d. 2 ¼

37. If $2^4 = 4^x$, then $x =$
    a. 2
    b. 4
    c. 6
    d. 8

38. If $2x + 3y = 13$ and $4x - y = 5$, then $3x + 2y =$
    a. 2
    b. 3
    c. 6
    d. 12

39. A rectangle is divided into two squares, each with a perimeter of 20. What is the perimeter of the rectangle?
    a. 20
    b. 30
    c. 40
    d. 50

40. For what real number x is it true that $3(2x - 10) = x$?
    a. -6
    b. -5
    c. 5
    d. 6

41. A two-digit number is chosen at random. What is the probability that the chosen number is a multiple of 7?
    a. 1/10
    b. 1/9
    c. 11/90
    d. 13/90

42. If the measures of the three angles in a triangle are 2 : 6 : 10, what is the measure of the smallest angle?
    a. 20 degrees
    b. 40 degrees
    c. 60 degrees
    d. 80 degrees

43. Henry is three times as old as Truman. Two years ago, Henry was five times as old as Truman. How old is Henry now?
    a. 4
    b. 8
    c. 12
    d. 16

44. If $a = 3$ and $b = -2$, what is the value of $a^2 + 3ab - b^2$?
    a. 5
    b. -13
    c. -4
    d. -20

45. Factor the following expression: $x^2 + x - 12$
    a. $(x - 4)(x + 4)$
    b. $(x - 2)(x + 6)$
    c. $(x + 6)(x - 2)$
    d. $(x + 4)(x - 3)$

46. The average of six numbers is 4. If the average of two of those numbers is 2, what is the average of the other four numbers?
    a. 5
    b. 6
    c. 7
    d. 8

47. How many 3-inch segments can a 4.5-yard line be divided into?
    a. 15
    b. 45
    c. 54
    d. 64

48. If $a = 4$, $b = 3$, and $c = 1$, then $\dfrac{a(b-c)}{b(a+b+c)} =$

    a. 4/13
    b. 1/3
    c. 1/4
    d. 1/6

Application of Mathematics Skills and Knowledge to Classroom Instruction

49. A student is asked to find the mode of the following set: {2, 4, 5, 6, 6, 7}.
The student's answer is 5. What has the student most likely done wrong?
    a. The student has excluded the greatest and least values in the set.
    b. The student has included both sixes in his calculation.
    c. The student has found the mean instead of the mode.
    d. The student has found the median instead of the mode.

50. Students are asked to convert 3/5 into a decimal. What is one possible first step?
    a. Multiply numerator and denominator by two
    b. Divide denominator by numerator
    c. Multiply numerator by denominator
    d. Raise denominator to the third power

51. $5(2 + 4) \div 2 = ?$
A student composes the number sentence above in response to the following problem:
"Divide the sum of the products of 5 and 2 and 5 and 4 by 2."
How else could the student have written this number sentence?
    a. $2 \div 5 \times 2 + 5 \times 4 = ?$
    b. $5 + 2 \times 5 + 4 \div 4 = ?$
    c. $5(2) + 5(4) \div 2 = ?$
    d. $5 + 2 \times 5 + 4 \div 2 = ?$

52. Students are given the following word problem:

- 43 -

"A jar of marbles contains six white marbles, eight black marbles, ten red marbles, and twelve green marbles. If John reaches into the jar and selects a marble, what are his chances of selecting a black one?"

Which of the following indicates a correct strategy for solving this problem?

    a. 8^4
    b. $(6 + 8 + 10 + 12)/8$
    c. $8(6 + 10 + 12)$
    d. $8/(6 + 8 + 10 + 12)$

53. Students are given the following problem: $4a - 3 = 17$. What should their first step be?
    a. Dividing both sides of the equation by four
    b. Subtracting seventeen from both sides of the equation
    c. Multiplying both sides of the equation by four
    d. Adding three to both sides of the equation

54. Students are asked to find the sum of the following set: 3, 5.67, 40.54, and 1.765. What precaution should students make when performing this calculation?
    a. Students should arrange the problem vertically, such that the decimal points are aligned.
    b. Students should round all of the terms to the tenths place.
    c. Students should ignore the decimal points in the terms and add a decimal point to the sum.
    d. Students should only add two terms at a time.

55. Students are given the following word problem:
"Andrea buys a shirt that is normally $24 but is being sold at a 20% discount. If Andrea pays a 5% sales tax on the shirt, what is the total cost?"
Identify the equation students should devise to solve this problem.
    a. $24 \times 1.2 \times 0.05$
    b. $[24 - (24 \times 0.2)] \times 1.05$
    c. $24 \times 0.2 \times 0.05$
    d. $24 - (24 \times 0.2) \times 1.05$

56. Students are asked to convert 5 2/7 into an improper fraction. Which operations will they need to perform?
    a. Multiplication and division
    b. Multiplication and addition
    c. Division and subtraction
    d. Division and addition

57. A student is presented with the following problem: $2(5 + 2) - 7^2 + 20$. Which operation(s) must the student perform before squaring seven?
    a. Multiply two across the parentheses
    b. Add the terms in parentheses
    c. Both A and B
    d. Neither A nor B

58. A student is asked to find the area of a triangle with a base of 5 and a height of 6. The student's answer is 30. What has the student most likely done wrong?

a. Nothing: the student's answer is correct.
b. Failed to multiply the product of 5 and 6 by 3
c. Failed to multiply the product of 5 and 6 by 1/2
d. Failed to multiply the product of 5 and 6 by 2

59. Students are given the following word problem:
"Vince asks for half of the remaining third of the peach pie. How much of a whole pie does Vince want?"
Which operation will students use to solve this problem?
a. Multiplication
b. Division
c. Addition
d. Subtraction

60. Students are asked to solve the following problem:
"Multiply the quotient of 6 and 2 by 4."
A student comes up with the incorrect answer of 48. What is the most likely cause of the student's error?
a. The student does not know the multiplication tables.
b. The student does not know the order of operations.
c. The student does not know the meaning of quotient.
d. The student does not know how to read.

Writing Skills and Knowledge

Questions 61-64: These questions present a sentence, all or part of which is underlined. Beneath each sentence you will find four ways of phrasing the underlined part. The first of these repeats the original; the other three are different. If you think the original is best, choose the first answer; otherwise, choose one of the other answers.

61. If he stops to consider the ramifications of this decision, it is probable that he will rethink his original decision a while longer.
a. it is probable that he will rethink his original decision.
b. he will rethink his original decision over again.
c. he probably will rethink his original decision.
d. he will most likely rethink his original decision for a bit.

62. "When you get older," she said "you will no doubt understand what I mean."
a. older," she said "you will no doubt
b. older" she said "you will no doubt
c. older," she said, "you will no doubt
d. older," she said "you will not

63. Dr. Anderson strolled past the nurses, examining a bottle of pills.
a. Dr. Anderson strolled past the nurses, examining a bottle of pills.

b. Dr. Anderson strolled past the nurses examining a bottle of pills.

c. Dr. Anderson strolled past, the nurses examining a bottle of pills.

d. Examining a bottle of pills, Dr. Anderson strolled past the nurses.

64. Karl and Henry <u>raced to the reservoir, climbed the ladder, and then they dove into</u> the cool water.

    a. raced to the reservoir, climbed the ladder, and then they dove into

    b. first raced to the reservoir, climbed the ladder, and then they dove into

    c. raced to the reservoir, they climbed the ladder, and then they dove into

    d. raced to the reservoir, climbed the ladder, and dove into

Questions 65-69: *Each sentence below has one or two blanks, each blank indicating that something has been omitted. For each question in this section, select the best answer from the choices provided.*

65. Because land is limited and the population is constantly growing, real estate _____ typically _____ over time.

    a. development ... falters

    b. values ... increase

    c. brokers ... compromise

    d. agents ... magnify

66. Infants and toddlers may sometimes have _____ sleep patterns due to growth spurts and rapid changes in their physical development.

    a. cohesive

    b. natural

    c. erratic

    d. fanciful

67. The maintenance workers handle quite a range of _____: irrigation repair, plumbing, and general maintenance.

    a. visitors

    b. flowers

    c. attractions

    d. responsibilities

68. Natural fibers like organic cotton and bamboo are _____ and _____ without the use of harsh chemicals.

    a. manufactured ... deployed

    b. woven ... filtered

    c. commissioned ... forgotten

    d. grown ... processed

69. _____ mattresses contain many toxic substances, such as flame-retardants, adhesives and chemical foams, which are not present in natural latex rubber.

    a. Conventional

    b. Queen-sized

    c. White

    d. Maximum

Question 70-74: *The following sentences test your ability to recognize grammar and usage errors. Each sentence contains either a single error or no error at all. No sentence contains more than one error. The error, if there is one, is lettered. If the sentence contains an error, select the one lettered part that must be changed to make the sentence correct. If the sentence is correct, select Choice E.*

70. (a.) <u>Being an honor student</u> with a (b.) <u>penchant with reading</u>, she (c.) <u>loves to</u> pick up a book during every spare (d.) <u>moment</u>. (e.) <u>NO ERROR</u>

71. At the (a.) <u>full arena</u>, (b.) <u>filled with</u> 15,000 concert-goers, the two friends (c.) <u>were still</u> somehow capable (d.)<u>to find</u> each other. (e.)<u>NO ERROR</u>

72. While the (a.)<u>TV anchorman</u> (b.)<u>relayed</u> the (c.)<u>details of</u> the storm, the family (d.)<u>fell</u> silent. (e.)<u>NO ERROR.</u>

73. I (a.)<u>had</u> already read (b.)<u>the book</u> (c.)<u>before</u>, so I knew what (d.)<u>to expect</u>. (e.)<u>NO ERROR</u>

74. The (a.) <u>entire staff</u> is (b.) <u>invited</u> to (c.)<u>Barbara Schneiders</u> retirement reception on Wednesday, Oct. 8 at 2:00 p.m. (d.)<u>in the community room</u>. (e.)<u>NO ERROR</u>

QUESTIONS 75-78 Refer to the following passage.
Picking the Perfect Pet
A
(1) Today's choices for pets go beyond the question of whether to get a cat or a dog? (2) Gerbils, rabbits, and amphibians is all popular options. (3) Before heading to an animal shelter, it is important to know what pet makes sense for your home or classroom. (4) An obvious question to answer if you rent is if pets are permitted. (5) Some apartment complex places weight and size limits on pets or charge fees. (6) If pets are permitted, more issues need to be considered.

75. Sentence 1: *"Today's choices for pets go beyond the question of whether to get a cat or a dog?"*
What correction should be made to this sentence?
    a. change the question mark to a period
    b. change Today's to Todays
    c. change question to questions
    d. change <u>whether</u> to <u>weather</u>

76. Sentence 2: *"Gerbils, rabbits, and amphibians is all popular options."*
What correction should be made to this sentence?
    a. remove the comma after Gerbils
    b. change amphibians to amfibians
    c. change is to are
    d. change <u>Gerbils</u> to <u>Hamsters</u>

77. Sentence 5: "*Some apartment complex places weight* and size limits on pets or charge fees."
Which of the following is the best way to write the underlined portion of this sentence? If you think the original is the best way to write the sentence, choose option 1..
    a. Some apartment complex places weight
    b. Some apartment complex places wait
    c. Some apartment complexes places weight
    d. Some apartment complexes place weight

78. Sentence (6): "*If pets are permitted, more issues need to be considered.*"
If you rewrote sentence (6) beginning with <u>More issues need to be considered,</u> the next words should be
    a. permitted pets
    b. if permitted
    c. are permitted
    d. if pets

Application of Writing Skills and Knowledge in Classroom Instruction

Questions 79 and 80 are based on the following rough draft written by a student.
    Fifteenth Birthday Parties
    By Juan
    (1) Last October, my sister turned fifteen. (2) When a girl turns fifteen where I am from (Mexico), her family has a big party for her and gives her a bunch of really nice presents. (3) My sister got some fancy jewelry and a new purse. (4) It was a nice day so we had the party under this really nice tent in the park. (5) All of my relatives came, even some that live really far away. (6) It was really nice of them to come. (7) When the party was almost over my sister was sort of sad because she knew that she would only have one party like this, but she was also really happy that all of the friends and family she loved were able to come.

79. What would be a better title for this essay?
    a. "Birthday Parties in Mexico"
    b. "A Family Holiday"
    c. "My Sister's Fifteenth Birthday Party"
    d. "Last October, My Sister Turned Fifteen"

80. What is one stylistic change the student might want to make?
    a. The student should tell the story from the perspective of his sister.
    b. The student should describe the presents in more detail.
    c. The student should get a direct quote from his sister.
    d. The student should use the word *really* less often.

81. A student's paper contains the following sentence:

Each of the players picked up their bronze trophy after winning the championship game.
The student has made an error of
  a. punctuation.
  b. spelling.
  c. grammar.
  d. diction.

82. A student's paper contains the following sentence:
Denise told us not to wait, which she said would put us behind schedule.
What must the student do to correct this sentence?
  a. Substitute a mistake that for which.
  b. Substitute that for which.
  c. Eliminate the comma.
  d. Correct the spelling of *schedule*.

83. A student's essay contains the following passage:
"After we went back into the kitchen, Mom told me the truth. Couldn't believe it, and I had to run upstairs and get my yearbook to check."
What is wrong with this passage as written?
  a. The second sentence is a run-on.
  b. The second sentence is a fragment.
  c. Yearbook should be two words.
  d. *Mom* should not be capitalized.

84. Which word is NOT spelled correctly?
  a. parallel
  b. abscence
  c. receive
  d. principle

85. A student's essay contains the following sentence:
Football players spend a great deal of time looking at video, it helps them prepare for the upcoming opponent.
What could the student do to correct this sentence?
  a. Place a hyphen in up-coming.
  b. Divide it into two sentences.
  c. Place an apostrophe in player's.
  d. Nothing, the sentence is correct as written.

86. Students are asked to write a letter to the newspaper editor. What word best describes the appropriate tone for this letter?
  a. measured
  b. amusing
  c. concerned
  d. cynical

87. A student's paper contains the following sentence:

Performers of this day in age know the truth: making a living in show business is tough.
The student has made an error of
    a. punctuation.
    b. spelling.
    c. grammar.
    d. diction.

88. A student's essay contains the following sentence:
I don't know any teachers that would allow such behavior.
What must the student do to correct this sentence?
    a. Substitute who for that.
    b. Place a comma after teachers.
    c. Substitute didn't for don't.
    d. Eliminate the word *any*.

Questions 89 and 90 are based on the following rough draft written by a student.
    My Favrit Day
    By Tom
    (1) My favret day and I wak up in my bed and go to the kichen an my mem has mad some pancaks. (2) I relly luv these pancaks thet my mom maks and she knows how to mak them the best way. (3) When I go otside all my frens is there and we rid biks around the blokc and then go over the park and paly basketbal. (4) This is my favrit day but yurs mite be diffrnet. (5) When I go hom later my dad is ther and we throw around the ball and go ot fer ice cream.

89. What would be a better way of phrasing the first sentence?
    a. It's my favorite day, and I wake up in my bed and go to the kitchen to eat my mom's pancakes.
    b. I eat my mom's pancakes in the kitchen after I get out of bed on my favorite day.
    c. My favorite day begins when I wake up in my bed and go to the kitchen to eat the pancakes my mom has made.
    d. My favorite day begins in the kitchen with mom's pancakes.

90. Which two sentences should be switched to improve this essay?
    a. 1 and 2
    b. 4 and 5
    c. 2 and 4
    d. 1 and 3

Answers and Explanations

Reading Skills and Knowledge

1. C: The sentence reads, "Your brain <u>filters</u> [your nose] out," which means your brain ignores it.

2. B: Only choice B reflects the meaning of the term "retina," which is a part of the eye's anatomy.

3. B: The final sentence reads, "Your brain works hard to make the world look continuous." It follows that visual perception is an active process, not a passive one, making choice B the best answer.

4. A: If the reader follows the instructions given in the paragraph, the O and X in the middle of the passage can be used to demonstrate the blind spot in the visual field.

5. B: The passage explains the way that visual perception works.

6. D: Much of the information in the passage is provided to show examples of how the brain fills in gaps in the visual field.

7. A: The author of the passage mentions the nose to demonstrate how the brain filters information out of the visual field.

8. B: Choice B can be inferred from the second paragraph. The paragraph states that the brain filters out information, which means that the brain does not perceive all activity in the visual field.

9. B: The meaning of this term can be found in the context of the sentence. Choice B, "stays in the sky all night," is closest in meaning to the statement "so it can be seen all night long."

10. D: This passage's purpose is to inform the reader of different interpretations of this group of stars.

11. A: Only choice A can be correctly inferred from the third paragraph.

12. C: Only choice C is consistent with the meaning of the passage.

13. C: Choice C is closest to the meaning of the passage.

14. C: Choice C best captures the way the passage uses the term <u>code</u>.

15. D: Though several of these statements are true, only choice D is directly related to the passage itself.

16. B: Choice B best captures the meaning of the final paragraph.

17. D: The work is important because "it is often viewed as the first significant work of English literature."

18. D: This can be concluded based on the section of the passage that states "Today, with blogs, virtually anybody can put their work out there for others to view. It's as easy as setting up your blog, naming it, and posting anything you want."

Application of Reading Skills and Knowledge to Classroom Instruction

19. D: Rate, accuracy, and prosody. Fluent readers are able to read smoothly and comfortably at a steady pace (rate). The more quickly a child reads, the greater the chance of leaving out a word or substituting one word for another (for example, *sink* instead of *shrink*). Fluent readers are able to maintain accuracy without sacrificing rate. Fluent readers also stress important words in a text, group words into rhythmic phrases, and read with intonation (prosody).

20. C: Fail, producing students at a Frustration reading level. Those reading below grade level are likely to give up entirely. Those reading at grade level are likely to get frustrated and form habits that will actually slow down their development. Giving students texts that are too far beyond their reach produces frustrated readers. In an effort to succeed, frustrated writers are likely to apply strategies that have worked for them in the past but cannot work in this case because the text is simply beyond them. Looking for contextual clues to understand the meaning of unfamiliar words requires that most of the words in the passage are familiar. Breaking unfamiliar words into individual phonemes or syllables can be effective, but not if the number of such words is excessive. In this case, students below reading level and students at reading level will become frustrated when the skills that have worked for them in the past now fail.

21. C: Tier-two words. Tier-two words are words that are used with high frequency across a variety of disciplines or words with multiple meanings. They are characteristic of mature language users. Knowing these words is crucial to attaining an acceptable level of reading comprehension and communication skills.

22. C: Reading at her Independent reading level. When reading independently, students are at the correct level if they read with at least 97% accuracy.

23. B: To correct an error in reading a student has made, specifically clarifying where and how the error was made so that the student can avoid similar errors in the future. A reading teacher offers corrective feedback to a student in order to explain why a particular error in reading is, in fact, an error. Corrective feedback is specific; it locates where and how the student went astray so that similar errors can be avoided in future reading.

24. C: Content-specific words. Because these words are specific to paleontology, it's unlikely the students know their meanings. Without understanding what these words mean, the

students would not be able to understand the content of the passage they were about to read.

25. B: Prior knowledge is knowledge the student brings from previous life or learning experiences to the act of reading. It is not possible for a student to fully comprehend new knowledge without first integrating it with prior knowledge. Prior knowledge, which rises from experience and previous learning, provides a framework by which new knowledge gained from the act of reading can be integrated. Every act of reading enriches a student's well of prior knowledge and increases that student's future ability to comprehend more fully any new knowledge acquired through reading.

26. C: She is reading at an Instructional level. In one minute, a student who misreads one or less than one word per twenty words, or with 95%–100% accuracy, is at an Independent reading level. A student who misreads one or less than one word per ten words, or with 90%–95% accuracy, is at an Instructional level. A student misreading more than one word out of ten, or with less than 90% accuracy, is at a Frustration level.

27. A: Nothing. These children are simply at an early stage in the reading/writing process. When emergent readers become aware of the connections between letters and sounds, and between reading and writing, they want to practice the skills they see proficient readers use. While a proficient writer knows that letters are grouped into words and that words are constructed into sentences that move from left to right and from the top of the page to the bottom, an emergent reader/writer knows only that letters magically contain sounds that other people can read. It is necessary for children to pass through early stages in which they scribble-write and pretend they are scripting letters, which leads to a stage in which they actually do write the initial letter of a word all over the page. Next, the emergent reader/writer will write the initial letter of many of the words that belong in the sentence and will write them sequentially. KJM, for example, might mean *the cat chased a mouse.*

28. C: Right and left; left. Researchers have discovered through brain imaging that a dyslexic reader uses both sides of the brain. Non-dyslexic readers use only the left side.

29. C: Persuasive. The author is hoping to persuade or convince young readers to avoid sex by providing them with facts as well as by using rhetorical devices such as dispelling opposing arguments.

30. C: Write a compound word such as *doghouse* on the board. Underline *dog,* and then *house.* Beneath the words draw a picture of a dog and a house, joined with a plus sign. Next, write another compound word and ask the class to draw the pictures in their journals. Give the students a handout with several compound words. Ask them to underline the two words, then to draw the pictures. Students will discover that compound words are composed of two distinct words that in combination mean something new but related.

Mathematics Skills and Knowledge

31. C: The decrease was the difference between 14,000 and 12,600: 1400. 1400 is 10% of 14,000.

32. A: 30% of 50 is determined by multiplying 30/100 x 50. The answer is 15. Then, we need to find the number that 15 is 50% (or ½) of. This can be found by using the equation $15 = 1/2x$. $x = 30$.

33. B: The average of 7 and x is 7 + x divided by 2. The average of 9, 4, and x is 9 + 4 + x divided by 3. $(7+x)/2 = (9+4+x)/3$. Simplify the problem and eliminate the denominators by multiplying the first side by 3 and the second side by 2. For the first equation, (21 + 3x)/6. For the second equation, (18 + 8 + 2x)/6. Since the denominators are the same, they can be eliminated, leaving $21 + 3x = 26 + 2x$. Solving for x gets $x = 26-21$. $x = 5$.

34. D: This is a simple average problem. If x denotes Annie's score, 86+98+90+x, divided by 4 equals 92. To solve, multiply each side by 4 and add the known scores together to get 274 + x = 368. Subtract 274 from 368 to solve for x. $x = 94$.

35. D: If $3x - 2 = 1$, then $3x = 3$. Therefore, $x = 1$.

36. B: Determine what the ratio of vinegar to the salad dressing as a whole is. Vinegar is ¼ of a cup and the salad dressing as a whole is ¼ cup vinegar plus ¾ cup oil, or 1 cup. Thus, vinegar is ¼ of the salad dressing. Therefore, ¼ of 6 cups is 3/2 or 1 ½ cups of vinegar.

37. A: $2^4 = 2 \times 2 \times 2 \times 2 = 16$. Therefore, $4^x = 16$; $x = 2$.

38. D: Solving for y in the second equation gives $y = 4x-5$. If we plug this into the first equation we get $2x + 3(4x-5) = 13$. Solving for this equation gives us $14x = 28$, or $x = 2$. Then, plug the value of x into either equation to solve for y. $y = 3$. Therefore, $3x + 2y = 12$.

39. B: The perimeter of a square is four times the length of any one of its sides. If a square's perimeter is 20, the length of any side is 5. The perimeter of this rectangle is six times the length of a side, which is 30.

40. D: To solve $3(2x - 10) = x$, first multiply the left side out. $6x - 30 = x$. Therefore, $5x = 30$, and $x = 6$.

41. D: There are 90 two-digit numbers (all integers from, and including, 10 to, and including, 99). Of those, there are 13 multiples of 7: 14, 21, 28, 35, 42, 49, 56, 63, 70, 77, 84, 91, 98.

42. A: The sum of the measures of the three angles of any triangle is 180. The equation of the angles of this triangle can be written as $2x + 6x + 10x = 180$, or $18x = 180$. Therefore, x = 10. Therefore, the measure of the smallest angle is 20.

43. C: If t equals Truman's age now, and 3t equals Henry's age now, t-2 equals Truman's age two years ago and 3t-2 equals Henry's age two years ago. Since Henry was 5 times as old as Truman two years ago, we can solve for $3t-2 = 5(t-2)$. Solving this gives us $3t-2 = 5t-10$ or $2t = 8$. Therefore, t = 4. Since Henry is three times as old as Truman, Henry is 12.

44. B: Simply substitute the given values for *a* and *b* and perform the required operations.

45. D: To solve this problem, work backwards. That is, perform FOIL on each answer choice until you derive the original expression.

46. A: A set of six numbers with an average of 4 must have a collective sum of 24. The two numbers that average 2 will add up to 4, so the remaining numbers must add up to 20. The average of these four numbers can be calculated: 20/4 = 5.

47. C: There are 12 inches in a foot and 3 feet in a yard. Four and a half yards is equal to 162 inches. To determine the number of 3-inch segments, divide 162 by 3.

48. B: Substitute the given values and solve. Resolve the parenthetical operations first.

Application of Mathematics Skills and Knowledge to Classroom Instruction

49. C: The student has found the mean instead of the mode. The mean, or average, is the sum of the terms in the set divided by the number of terms. In this case, that calculation would look like this: $(2 + 4 + 5 + 6 + 6 + 7) \div 6 = 5$. The mode, however, is the term used most often in a number set. In this set, 6 is the only number that appears more than once, and is therefore the mode.

50. A: One possible first step for this problem would be to multiply the numerator and denominator by two. A fraction can be easily converted into a decimal if the denominator ends in a power of ten. Since the denominator of 3/5 is five, multiplying both numerator and denominator will yield an equivalent fraction of 6/10, or six tenths. This is easily converted into the decimal 0.6. The more traditional method for converting a fraction into a decimal is to divide the numerator by the denominator (the opposite of the operation described in answer choice B).

51. C: The student could have also composed his number sentence as $5(2) + 5(4) \div 2 = ?$ According to the distributive property of multiplication, $5(2 + 4) = 5 \times 2 + 5 \times 4$. Remember that many problems can be arranged correctly as several different number sentences. The important consideration is to arrange the number sentence such that it will be performed in the proper order. In this problem, the sequence should be multiplication, addition, division.

52. D: The expression $8/(6 + 8 + 10 + 12)$ indicates a good strategy for solving this problem. The word problem asks students to determine the probability of finding a black marble in a jar containing several different colors of marble. The best way to find the answer is to set up a fraction with the number of black marbles in the numerator and the total number of marbles in the denominator. When this fraction is arranged, it will look like answer choice B. The expression simplifies to $8/36 = 2/9$, meaning that there is a 2 in 9 chance of selecting a black marble.

53. D: The student's first step should be adding three to both sides of the equation. Solving a simple algebraic equation of this type requires isolating the variable on one side. This process could begin by dividing each side by four (thus eliminating the coefficient from $4a$), but this would be much more complicated than simply adding three to both sides. Students should be trained to resolve this type of equation in the easiest way possible. Adding three to both sides yields an equation of $4a = 20$, which, once both sides are divided by four, leaves $a = 5$.

54. A: When performing this calculation, students should arrange the terms vertically, such that the decimal points are aligned. It is easy for students to get confused when performing addition or subtraction with groups of numbers that have varying amounts of digits to the right of the decimal point. The best way to arrange such a problem is vertically. Students will also find it easier to perform this calculation if they add zeroes where necessary to give each number the same length to the right of the decimal point. In this problem, then, the terms would become 3.000, 5.670, 40.540, and 1.765.

55. B: Students should use the equation [24 – (24 × 0.2)] × 1.05 to solve this problem. The problem requires students to calculate the sale price of the shirt and then add the sales tax. The discounted price is calculated by subtracting the amount of the discount (24 × 0.2) from the original price of the shirt (24). This operation is placed in brackets so that it will be completed before moving on to the second part of the problem, adding the sales tax. The sales tax is described as 5%, which is expressed as a decimal 0.05. However, the total price will include the discounted shirt price as well as 5% of that price in sales tax, so the total price must be calculated by multiplying the discounted price of the shirt by 1.05.

56. B: Students will need to perform multiplication and addition in order to convert 5 2/7 into an improper fraction. Converting a mixed number into an improper fraction is a relatively simple operation. The whole number, five in this case, is multiplied by the denominator (seven). The product (35) is then added to the numerator, yielding an improper fraction of 37/7. A fraction is described as improper when the numerator is larger than the denominator.

57. C: The student must first multiply two across the parentheses and then add the terms in the parentheses before squaring seven. This problem requires knowledge of the order of operations: parentheses, exponents, multiplication, division, addition, subtraction. Some students may find it easier to remember the order of operations if the initials with a mnemonic like "Please Excuse My Dear Aunt Sally," in which the first letters of the words are the same as for the operations.

58. C: The student has most likely failed to multiply the product of 5 and 6 by 1/2. The equation for finding the area of a triangle is $A = 1/2bh$. It appears that the student has multiplied the base and height of this triangle but has neglected to multiply by 1/2.

59. A: Students will use multiplication to solve this problem. This word problem requires students to perform fraction multiplication. Vince wants 1/2 of 1/3, which can be calculated 1/2 × 1/3 = 1/6. The answer, then, is that Vince wants 1/6 of a whole pie. Remember that the multiplication of fractions does not require a common denominator.

60. C: The most likely cause of the student's error is that she does not know the meaning of *quotient*. A student would arrive at the incorrect answer of 48 if she multiplied 6, 2, and 4. This is most likely the student's mistake. A quotient is the answer to a division problem. The quotient of 6 and 2 is 3, which multiplied by 4 yields the correct answer of 12.

Writing Skills and Knowledge

61. C: The original sentence is redundant and wordy.

62. C: The syntax of the original sentence is fine, but a comma after *said* but before the open-quotation mark is required.

63. D: In the original sentence, the modifier is placed too far away from the word it modifies.

64. D: The verb structure should be consistent in a sentence with parallel structures.

65. B: The word "because" at the beginning of the sentence indicates that a reason is being given for the condition described in the second clause. Answer B logically completes the sentence: increasing demand for a limited resource leads to an increase in its value.

66. C: The second part of the sentence suggests that growth spurts and rapid physical changes disturb sleep patterns, so they are not likely to be "natural." Of the remaining choices, only "erratic" makes sense, and it provides a good description of a disturbed pattern.

67. D: The list that follows clearly describes tasks for which maintenance workers may be responsible as part of their jobs.

68. D: The sentence describes the advantages of natural organic fibers for the consumer. Choice D describes the steps required to bring them to market.

69. A: The sentence contrasts the properties of typical, or "conventional", mattresses with natural ones. The properties listed obviously have no connection with mattress size or color.

70. B: Penchant with reading is an incorrect idiom. If you say it out loud, you will find that it does not sound right. It should be penchant *for* reading.

71. D: To be read correctly, it should say *of finding*. The word *capable* is the key here. If the sentence had said *able to find*, it would have been correct. But the adjective *capable* is generally followed by *of*.

72. E: There is no error in this sentence.

73. C: Since the sentence uses the word *already*, the use of the word *before* is redundant. Either the word *already* or the word *before* should be taken out, and *already* was not a choice of something that could or should be changed.

74. C: There should be an apostrophe before the *s* at the end of Barbara Schneider's name to show possession. The retirement reception belongs to her, so the correct way to write it should be: *Barbara Schneider's*.

75. A: The sentence is declarative, rather than interrogative, despite the implied question that is asked. It, therefore, requires a period as end mark. Choice B is not correct; the apostrophe is necessary to indicate possessive. Choice C., likewise, is incorrect; it does not solve the problem, and it creates a problem of agreement. Option D. is not correct; it offers a false homonym choice, which is not the problem and only compounds the error.

76. C: The sentence contains a disagreement between the compound subject, which is considered plural, and the singular verb. Changing *is* to *are* solves the problem. Choice A is incorrect; the comma is needed for items in a series. Choice B is not correct; the word is correctly spelled as written. Choice D, likewise, is incorrect; it offers only a cosmetic change, not a solution to the problem of subject-verb agreement.

77. D: The problem in the sentence as written is one of subject-verb agreement and colloquial or substandard English. *Some* indicates that more than one apartment complex is being discussed. It, therefore, is necessary to change both the subject and verb to plural. Choice A is incorrect; the sentence as written clearly contains an error to be remedied. Choice B is not correct; choosing an alternative spelling for the homonym does not solve the problem. Choice C is incorrect as well; it creates instead a different subject-verb agreement problem.

78. D: The question tests students on sentence reconstruction, placing the independent clause, rather than the dependent clause, first. The first words of the dependent clause, *if pets*, must, therefore, come first. Choice A. is incorrect; building a phrase around these two words is grammatically impossible. Choice B. is also not correct; one cannot create a clause from such a beginning. Option C is incorrect as well; beginning with the verb is not a good choice.

Application of Writing Skills and Knowledge in Classroom Instruction

79. C: "My Sister's Fifteenth Birthday Party" would be a better title for this essay. The student's title, "Fifteenth Birthday Parties," is much too vague and gives the impression that the essay will be about these special parties in general, when in fact it is about one party in particular. A title should be as specific as possible without failing to encompass every part of the text. The other answer choices are either too vague (A and B) or specific (D).

80. D: The student should use the word *really* less often. This word is used five times in the essay. Like *very* and *pretty*, *really* is intended to add emphasis but is too vague and bland. It should be used rarely except in direct quotation, since it is a common conversational placeholder. Students should be taught to weigh the value of each word in their writing, and to eliminate those words that take up space without adding meaning.

81. C: The student has made an error of grammar. The subject of the sentence is the singular *each*, so the plural possessive pronoun *their* is incorrect. Instead, the student should substitute *his, her,* or *his or her*. This is a common error in writing and speech.

82. A: To correct this sentence, the student must substitute *a mistake that* for *which*. As originally written, the sentence has an unclear pronoun. It is difficult to determine the reference for *which*. Making the recommended substitution clarifies the sentence.

83. B: The second sentence of this passage is a fragment. It may seem strange to call this sentence a fragment, since it includes both subjects and verbs, but it does have a subject in the initial clause. The sentence would be correct if written, "I couldn't believe it, and I had to run upstairs and get my yearbook to check." *Yearbook* is always one word, and *Mom* should

- 58 -